Nelson's Victory

101 Questions & Answers about HMS Victory,
Nelson's Flagship at Trafalgar 1805

by

Peter Goodwin
MPhil, IEng & MIMarE

CONWAY MARITIME PRESS

Victory in No 2 Dock flying Nelson's signal 'England expects every man to do his duty', Trafalgar Day 1928. The three funnelled ship to the left is a Kent class light cruiser, to the right is the battleship Hood. By kind permission of the Commanding Officer HMS Victory

Copyright © Peter Goodwin, 2000

First published as *Countdown to Victory* in Great Britain in 2000 by
Manuscript Press, Portsmouth, England

This hardback edition published 2004 by Conway Maritime Press

A division of Anova Books
151 Freston Road
London W10 6TH
www.conwaymaritime.com
www.anovabooks.com

Reprinted 2005, 2006

British Library Cataloguing in Publication Data.
A catalogue record for this book is available from the British Library

ISBN 10:   0 85177 988 3
ISBN 13:   9 780851 779881

Printed in China

To Katy

Most works relating to *Victory* offer either too much or too little information. I hope *Nelson's Victory: 101 Questions & Answers about HMS Victory* finds the middle ground - satisfying without overwhelming readers with detail.

Naturally I could not have produced this work without the kind assistance of friends, colleagues and institutions. Foremost, I express my gratitude to Lieutenant Commander Frank Nowosielski, RN, the commanding officer of *Victory*, for encouraging this work and permitting me to use photographs and material held in the *Victory* archive. I thank Allison Wareham, Librarian of the Admiralty Library, Matthew Sheldon, Curator of the Royal Naval Museum and Matthew Little, Librarian of the Royal Marines Museum for providing information and primary documents held in their collections.

I would also like to thank the Trustees of the Royal Naval Museum, Portsmouth City Museum and Records Service, the Royal Marines Museum and *The News*, Portsmouth, for the reproduction of images contained within this book; the Nelson Society, the 1805 Club and, particularly the staff of the Public Record Office. I express my sincere gratitude to Dr Ann Coats and Dave London of Manuscript Press. Not only have they kindly undertaken the publication of this book, but their advice and direction has been extremely helpful.

Last and most important, I thank my partner Katy Ball for her dedication, support, patience and invaluable assistance in creating this book.

Peter Goodwin
August 2000

Lord Nelson in his cabin   Illustration by W Stacey

Contents

Nelson, Trafalgar & Victory   73

Victory after Trafalgar   81

'Save the Victory' campaign & restoration   85

Victory today: commissioned ship & public attraction   91

Endnotes   94

About the author   96

Bibliography   98

Victory moored in Portsmouth Harbour circa 1886 looking at Gosport; to the left is the two-masted training brig Martin. The large building to the right is the sail loft owned by Lapthorne, destroyed by bombing during World War II

Courtesy of Portsmouth City Museum & Records Service

A short history of *Victory*

HMS *Victory* is the only surviving 'line of battle' ship from the French revolutionary and Napoleonic wars. She served as Lord Nelson's flagship at the decisive battle of Trafalgar in 1805. However, her career commenced some forty years before. Ordered by the Navy Board on 6 June 1759 during the Seven Years' War, this first rate one hundred gun ship was designed by the Surveyor of the Navy, Sir Thomas Slade. Construction commenced at Chatham Dockyard on the 23 July 1759 under Master Shipwright John Lock and was completed by Edward Allin (Lock died in 1762). The year 1759, *annus mirabilis* or 'year of victories',[1] was the turning point of the war for Britain. Victories were won at Quebec, Minden, Lagos and Quiberon Bay - where Hawke, in a rising gale, drove and smashed the French fleet. These facts may well have been instrumental in naming the vessel. The year 1759 was also when Pitt the Younger, later to become England's leader in her war against revolutionary France, was born and William Boyce wrote the song 'Hearts of Oak'. Ironically, 1759 was also the year James Watt invented a steam engine with a separate condenser. Within seventy years his innovation brought about the demise of the sailing man of war.

The ship was officially christened *Victory* on 30 October 1760. In 1763 the Treaty of Paris ended the war and work on *Victory* was reduced. Her cost, when launched on 7 May 1765, amounted to £63,176. After initial sea trials *Victory* was put into ordinary[2] until France joined the War of American Independence. Commissioned in February 1778, she became the flagship of Admiral Augustus Keppel. On the 23 July Keppel fought an indecisive battle against d'Orvilliers off Ushant. For the next three years *Victory* served as flagship for Admirals Hardy, Geary, Drake and Parker. In March 1780, *Victory* was sheathed with copper plating to combat shipworm and marine growth. This innovation also improved her speed.

Under the flag of Admiral Richard Kempenfelt, *Victory* fell in with a French fleet off Ushant on 13 December 1781. The French, bound from Brest to

1

the West Indies, were escorting a convoy of troopships. Although Kempenfelt's squadron was numerically inferior, he captured the entire convoy from under the escort's noses. In October 1782, under the flag of Admiral Richard Howe, she took part in action off Cape Spartel and the relief of Gibraltar. After the war she was refitted in March 1783 at a cost of £15,372 19s 9d. At this stage her quarter deck armament was modified, 6 pounder guns being replaced with 12 pounders. Her sides, previously painted 'bright' with rosin[3] above the lower deck ports, were now painted a dull yellow ochre. The area below remained black. In 1787 she underwent a 'large repair' costing £37,523 17s 1d. Re-commissioned in 1789 under Howe, she became the flagship of Lord Hood the following year.

Storm clouds were gathering over Europe. In 1789 France was hurled into a bloody revolution whose outcome devastated Europe. With Britain's entry into the war in 1793, *Victory* became the flagship of Lord Samuel Hood who was appointed commander-in-chief of the Mediterranean fleet. While blockading Toulon she captured or destroyed several French ships and in July took part in the siege of San Fiorenzo, Calvi and Bastia on the island of Corsica. It was at Calvi that a promising young captain, Horatio Nelson, first came to the public's attention - leading a daring amphibious assault - but losing the sight of his right eye.

In 1794 *Victory* returned to Plymouth. Hood, his health shattered, lowered his flag. After another refit, she returned to the Mediterranean to become the flagship of Rear-Admiral Robert Man. In July 1795 *Victory* led the offensive in the unsuccessful action off Hyères where Vice-Admiral William Hotham failed to engage the Toulon fleet fully. As a result, Britain abandoned the Mediterranean. Nelson played a minor but distinguished role in this battle, commanding the sixty-four gun *Agamemnon*. After a brief command under Vice-Admiral Robert Linzee, Sir John Jervis hoisted his flag in *Victory* in the following December. On 14 February 1797, off Cape St Vincent, he led *Victory* with fourteen ships of the line against a Spanish squadron of twenty-seven ships under Admiral Don José de Cordoba. A decisive victory came largely as a result of Nelson's initiative. Now a commodore in the seventy-four gun *Captain*, he quit the line of battle and cut off the enemy's escape. He engaged, boarded and captured the massive 112 gun *San Josef*. Using this ship as his 'patent boarding bridge', he then captured the neighbouring eighty gun *San Nicholas*. With this action Sir John Jervis became Earl St Vincent and Nelson earned a knighthood and promotion to rear-admiral.

In October 1797 *Victory* returned to England and was surveyed at Portsmouth. Now thirty-two years old and battle-weary, she was sent to Chatham to await her fate. On 8 December, considered unfit for service, *Victory* was ordered to be converted into a hospital ship and ultimate dis-

Admiral Lord Horatio Nelson, KB[4]

posal. Fate intervened when, on 8 October 1799, the first rate *Impregnable* was lost in Chichester Harbour, creating an urgent need for another three-decked ship in the Channel fleet. Consequently *Victory* was given a new lease of life. A survey revealed that she was 'in want of a middling repair' at an estimate of £23,500.

Refitting commenced at Chatham in late 1800. Closer inspection stressed considerable disorder. Various parts of the hull required rebuilding, over sixty *per cent* of her knees needed refastening or replacing and many port lids needed refitting. To comply with recent improvements, her open stern galleries were removed and the entire stern was closed in. Two extra ports were cut on her lower gun deck and the magazines were lined in copper, conforming with contemporary practice. The heavy ornate figurehead, now rotten, was replaced with the simpler, lighter design as presently fitted. This, together with reduced ornate work on the stern, corresponded to the latest regulations on carving expenses. Composite masts, furnished with iron hoops, replaced her pole masts. The ship was also repainted with the black and yellow livery as seen today. The port lids were later painted black, producing the much imitated 'Nelson chequer' pattern.

By March 1801 war had exhausted Britain and France, while political pressure over Catholic emancipation had forced Prime Minister Pitt to resign on 5 February. Nelson, turning a 'blind eye' to Admiral Hyde Parker's order to withdraw, crushed the Danes at the battle of Copenhagen on 2 April 1801, thereby destroying the Northern League and thwarting Napoleon's ambitions. The new government under Henry Addington negotiated the fragile and short-lived Peace of Amiens with France. Peace was signed on 27 March 1802. Less urgent work on *Victory* continued until she was finally undocked on 11 April 1803. The repairs now amounted to £70,933, more than twice the original estimate. All her heavy lower deck 42 pounder guns were replaced with lighter and more manageable 32 pounders.

Under her new captain, Thomas Masterman Hardy, *Victory* sailed for Portsmouth on 14 May 1803. Two days later, hostilities with France reopened with the immediate threat of invasion. Four days later *Victory* sailed, carrying the Mediterranean's newly appointed commander-in-chief, Vice-Admiral Lord Nelson. From this point, Nelson and *Victory* became synonymous.

For the next eighteen months, Nelson blockaded the French fleet in Toulon to prevent it escaping to join force with other French or Spanish squadrons. Periodically, ships of Nelson's squadron would retire for repairs and re-provisioning to the safe anchorage of Agincourt Sound, Corsica. On such an occasion, on 18 April 1805, Nelson's frigates, the 'eyes' of his fleet, suddenly signalled that the Toulon fleet under Vice-Admiral Pierre Villeneuve had sailed. *Victory* weighed anchor immediately and the 'great chase' began that led *Victory* first eastward to Alexandria, then across the Atlantic and back. With no news, Nelson quitted the Mediterranean, passing through the Straits of Gibraltar on 4 May. Napoleon's invasion plan sent Villeneuve to the West Indies to draw the English from the Channel. Nelson's hot pursuit foiled his intentions. Nelson finally ran Villeneuve to ground at Cadiz where the combined French and Spanish fleet was blockaded. *Victory*, with an exhausted Nelson, dropped anchor at Spithead on 18 August. After a brief rest, Nelson sailed with *Victory* from Portsmouth on 15 September and joined the blockading fleet under Collingwood off Cadiz on the 28th.

Meanwhile Napoleon abandoned his invasion plans and marched troops based at Boulogne eastward to fight the Austrians. Villeneuve was ordered to take the combined Franco-Spanish fleet into the Mediterranean. On 18 October Nelson's frigates signalled that the enemy were weighing anchor. With a fleet of thirty-three ships of the line, Villeneuve made good his escape. Unable to shake off the pursuing British, however, he turned back for Cadiz and inevitable battle. As day broke on Monday 21 October 1805 off Cape Trafalgar, Nelson's fleet of twenty-seven ships formed into two columns and sailed towards the enemy. Battle commenced about 11.45 am with Collingwood's division breaching the rear of the combined fleet. Nelson in *Victory* followed shortly, driving into the van and opening a devastating broadside into the stern of Villeneuve's flagship *Bucentaure*. *Victory*

4

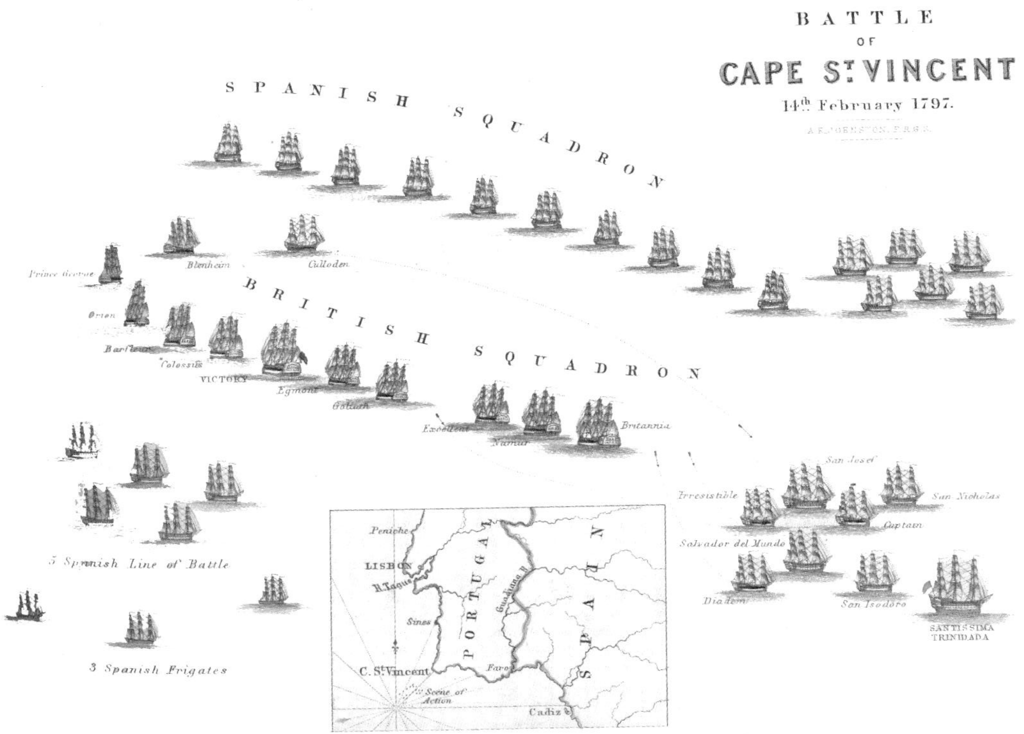

Battle of Cape St. Vincent, 14 February 1797; Victory, flagship of Admiral Sir John Jervis, appears seventh in the British line; Nelson's 74 gun Captain, is shown on the right engaging San Josef & San Nicholas

Napoleon Bonaparte[5]

next engaged and fell aboard *Rédoutable*. At about 1.15 pm, when fighting was at its fiercest, Nelson was shot by a French marksman, taken below and died at about 4.30 pm. As he lay dying, the combined fleet was routed and the Royal Navy won its greatest victory. Seventeen ships were captured and the French ship *Achille* blew up. This ended both the battle and any French challenge to Britain's naval supremacy.

Much damaged, *Victory* was towed to Gibraltar and finally returned to Portsmouth on 4 December, bearing her fallen hero. After repairs at Chatham costing £9,936, *Victory* was re-commissioned in March 1808 as the flagship of Admiral Saumarez, supporting the Swedes in the Baltic campaign. Next she was sent to Spain to evacuate the remnants of Sir John Moore's army from La Coruña, returning on 23 January 1809. April saw her back in the Baltic for the blockades of Kronstadt and Karlskrona. In 1811 she served under Rear-Admiral Sir Joseph Yorke, transporting reinforcements to Lisbon for Wellington's army in the Peninsula War. After further campaigns in the Baltic, she finally returned to Portsmouth on 4 December 1812 and was paid off sixteen days later.

Between 1814 and 1816 *Victory* was rebuilt with much alteration. The ornate beakhead bulkhead had been replaced with a more practical round bow, her bulwarks were built up square and her sides were painted with black and white horizontal stripes. The war with France at an end, she was placed

6

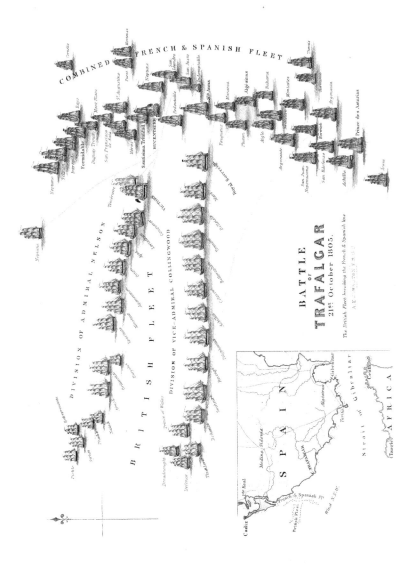

Battle of Trafalgar, 11.30 am, 21 October 1805; the British fleet, sailing line ahead in two columns, bears down on the combined fleet   *Naval Chronicle, xiv*

Reef Knot

back into ordinary, laid up in reserve. In 1824 *Victory* took on a new rôle as flagship for the Port Admiral and later tender to *Duke of Wellington*. In 1831 the ship was listed for disposal, but Hardy, now First Sea Lord, at his wife's request refused to sign the order and gave *Victory* a second reprieve. Refitted in 1888, she was re-coppered for the fifteenth and last time. The following year she became flagship for the commander-in-chief and remains so today.

Disaster struck in 1903 when she was accidentally rammed by *Neptune*, under tow to the breaker's yard. After emergency docking she went back to her familiar moorings. This event, together with the ensuing Trafalgar Centenary, raised questions about her future. However, World War I intervened. Finally, through a national appeal initiated by the Society for Nautical Research, *Victory* was put into her current dock on 12 January 1922 and restored to her 1805 appearance as a living monument to the Royal Navy ... Nelson's navy.

'Nelson is shot'   Courtesy of the Royal Marines Museum

Trafalgar Day during World War II: officers laying wreath on the quarter deck where Nelson fell
By kind permission of the Commanding Officer HMS *Victory*

Building & launching *Victory*

1. Why was Victory built?

Following continuous hostile attacks by the French and their Indian allies against British colonists in America, Britain declared war on France in 1756, begining the conflict known as the Seven Years' War. It was therefore necessary to increase the strength of the Royal Navy. Parliament voted to build twelve new ships of the line, one of which was to be a first rate of 100 guns, as yet unnamed. Timber to construct a first rate had been set aside to season at Chatham Dockyard fifteen years earlier.

2. When did Parliament authorise the building of Victory?

Navy estimates for 1759 were voted by Parliament on 18 December 1758.

3. How many naval ships have been named Victory?

There were five other ships bearing the same name. The first was a merchant vessel named *Christopher* which was purchased into the Navy in 1560 and renamed *Victory*. In 1586 she was rebuilt and listed as a ship of 800 tons with an armament of twelve 18 pounders, nine 6 pounders and twenty smaller guns. When she fought against the Spanish Armada in 1588 her complement comprised 300 mariners, 34 gunners and 400 soldiers. She was broken up in 1608.

The second *Victory* was a 42 gun ship of 870 tons designed by Phineas Pett and built at Deptford in 1620. In 1666 she was rebuilt at Chatham as a second rate of 82 guns and tonnage of 1,020 bm (builder's measurement). While in service she saw action against the Dutch off Dover in 1652, Portland, Gabbard and Scheveningen 1653, Orfordness 1666, Solebay 1672 and Texel in 1673. She also fought against the French at Barfleur in 1692. This ship was broken up at Woolwich in 1691.

The third, *Little Victory*, a fifth rate of 28 guns with a tonnage of 175 bm was built at Chatham in 1665 and expended as a fireship in 1671.

The fourth, *Victoire*, a fifth rate of 38 guns, was captured from the French on 5 April 1666 and later captured by the Dutch in 1672.

The fifth was a first rate of 100 guns laid down at Portsmouth on 23 February 1726 and launched on 23 February 1737. The dimensions of this ship were: length on the gun deck, 174 feet 6 inches; breadth, 50 feet 6 inches; and tonnage, 1,921 bm. This vessel was wrecked with a total loss of life on the Casquets on 5 October 1744. The origins of this *Victory* are noteworthy as she was technically a rebuild using the frames of *Royal James* which was built in 1675. The *Royal James* was renamed *Victory* in 1691, rebuilt at Chatham in 1695, renamed *Royal George* on the 27 October 1714 and again renamed *Victory* in September 1715. Unfortunately the ship was burnt by accident in 1721 and taken to pieces in April of the same year, the timbers being used for the *Victory* launched in 1737.

Oak trees were carefully selected to provide shaped components   Illustration by P Goodwin

THIS STONE
MARKS THE SITE OF
THE OLD SINGLE DOCK
CONSTRUCTED IN 1623
AND REPLACED IN 1858
BY THE PRESENT
№ 2 DOCK

Chatham Dockyard where Victory was built   Photograph by P Goodwin

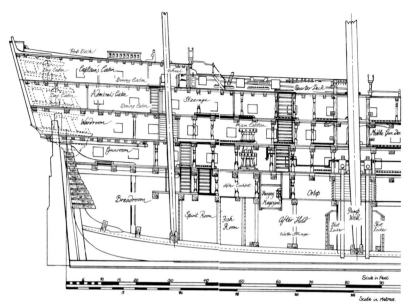

HMS Victory Inboard Profile

4. Who designed Victory?

Victory was designed by Sir Thomas Slade, Surveyor of the Navy, 1755-1771. His designs, largely adapted from captured French ships, were approved by the Board of Admiralty on 14 June 1759, authorising building to commence on 7 July.

5. Who built Victory & when did building begin?

The keel was laid in the old single dock at Chatham Dockyard on 23 July 1759, construction continuing for six years. Construction was first undertaken by John Lock, master shipwright at Chatham and, on his death in 1762, completed by his successor Edward Allin.

6. What are Victory's dimensions?

Length overall (figurehead to taffrail)	227 ft 6 in	69.34 m
Length on the gun deck	186 ft	56.70 m
Length of the keel for tonnage	152 ft 3 5/8 in	46.41 m
Moulded breadth	51 ft 6 in	15.70 m
Extreme breadth	51 ft 10 in	15.80 m
Depth in hold[6]	21 ft 6 in	6.55 m
Height of mainmast from waterline	205 ft	62.50 m
Burthen	2,162 tons	2,197 tonnes
Displacement	3,500 tons	3,556 tonnes
Draught afore	23 ft 9 in	7.24 m
Draught abaft	24 ft 5 in	7.44 m

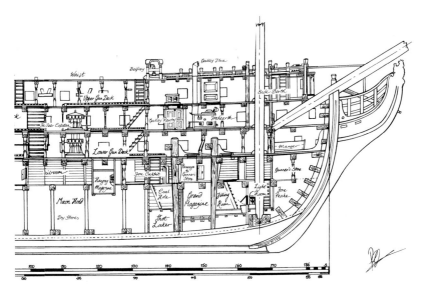

Illustration by P Goodwin

7. What types of wood were used for building Victory?

Elm was used for the keel and the lowermost strakes of the hull planking while good curved or 'compass' oak was used for her stempost, frames, knees and breasthooks, etc. Because of her size, the sternpost was made from one single oak tree. Straight oak (some imported from Danzig - modern Gdansk) was used for her beams, external planking and internal strengtheners. Oak was also used for the planking of the main, or lower gun deck. Fir was used for the planking of the upper decks and bulkheads - internal walls that subdivided the ship into compartments.

8. How much timber was used to build Victory?

Before conversion into shaped components, three hundred thousand cubic feet (8,444 cubic metres) was required to construct the hull. With one tree or load averaging fifty cubic feet (1.4 cubic metres), this volume equates to six thousand trees taken from about a hundred acres or forty hectares of woodland.[7] Of this figure some ninety *per cent* of the timber used was oak, mostly felled in the Wealden forests of Kent and Sussex.

9. How thick is the hull?

Near the keel the hull is a little under three feet (91.4 cm) thick. At this point, the frames or ribs are one foot eleven inches (58.4 cm), while at her waterline, the hull is about two feet six inches (76.2 cm) thick.

13

Cross-section of Victory at the mainmast

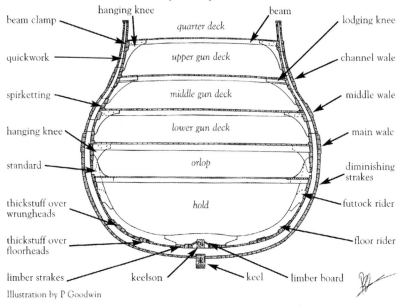

beam clamp · hanging knee · beam · lodging knee

quarter deck

quickwork · upper gun deck · channel wale

spirketting · middle gun deck · middle wale

hanging knee · lower gun deck · main wale

standard · orlop · diminishing strakes

thickstuff over wrungheads · hold · futtock rider

thickstuff over floorheads · floor rider

limber strakes · keelson · keel · limber board

Illustration by P Goodwin

10. How many copper plates were used to sheath the lower hull?

Approximately 3,923 copper plates were used to sheath the hull, each four feet (1.22 m) long and fourteen inches (35.56 cm) wide. Plating came in two sizes according to where it was used: 28 oz (0.79 kg) and 32 oz (0.91 kg) per square foot. The thinner plates weighed a little over eight pounds each while the heavier plates weighed nine and a third pounds. The sheathing plates were nailed to the hull planking with copper nails one and a half inches (3.8 cm) long and quarter of an inch (6.4 mm) in diameter. On average each plate was held with one hundred and forty nails, thus the total was approximately 549,220.

	Tons	Tonnes
Estimated total weight of copper plates	15.30	15.05
Estimated weight of nails - each 0.16oz (4.5g)	2.43	2.39
Total weight	17.73	17.45

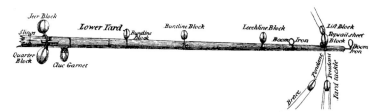

11. How were her masts & yards made?

Fir, pine or spruce were used for the masts, as this type of wood was both light and flexible. These timbers were imported from the Baltic States and Norway. When first built, each lower mast was made from a single tree three feet in diameter. This form of mast was called a 'pole mast'. Timber for pole masts was imported from New England, but the American War of Independence interrupted this supply. To resolve this problem, an alternative method of mast making, already used by the French, was adopted. Known as a 'composite mast', lower masts (main and fore) were manufactured, using between seven and nine smaller trees, carefully shaped and joined together to form the required diameter.

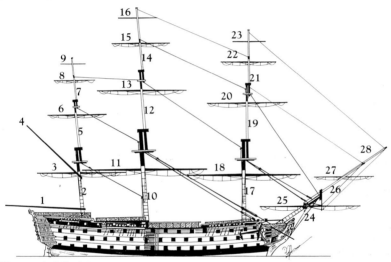

Illustration by P Goodwin

Masts & Yards

1. mizzen boom
2. mizzen mast
3. crossjack yard
4. mizzen gaff
5. mizzen topmast
6. mizzen topsail yard
7. mizzen topgallant mast
8. mizzen topgallant yard
9. mizzen royal yard

10. main mast
11. main yard
12. main topmast
13. main topsail yard
14. main topgallant mast
15. main topgallant yard
16. main royal yard

17. fore mast
18. fore yard
19. fore topmast
20. fore topsail yard
21. fore topgallant mast
22. fore topgallant yard
23. fore royal yard
24. bowsprit
25. spritsail yard
26. jibboom
27. sprit topsail yard
28. flying jibboom

15

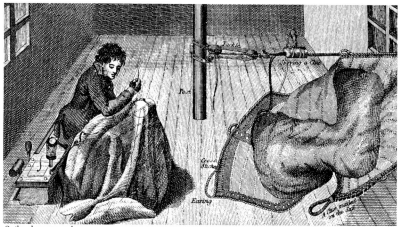

Sailmaker at work

Illustration by D Steel

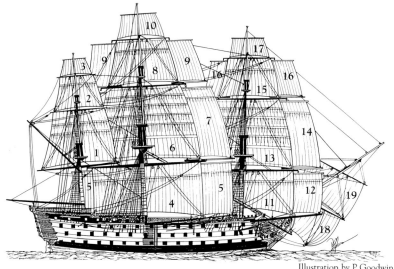

Illustration by P Goodwin

Square Sails:

1. mizzen topsail
2. mizzen topgallant
3. mizzen royal

4. main coarse
5. main lower studdingsails
6. main topsail
7. main topsail studdingsails
8. main topgallant
9. main topgallant studdingsails
10. main royal

11. fore coarse
12. fore lower studdingsails
13. fore topsail
14. fore topsail studdingsails
15. fore topgallant
16. fore topgallant studdingsails
17. fore royal
18. spritsail
19. sprit topsail

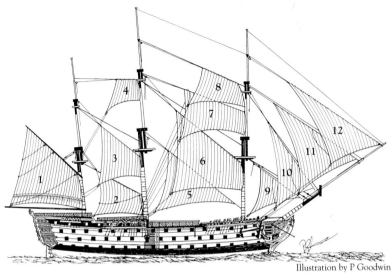

Illustration by P Goodwin

Fore & Aft Sails:

1. mizzen (spanker)
2. mizzen staysail
3. mizzen topmast staysail
4. mizzen topgallant staysail
5. main staysail
6. main topmast staysail
7. middle staysail
8. main topgallant staysail
9. fore staysail
10. fore topmast staysail
11. jib
12. flying jib

12. How much rope was used for her rigging?

Approximately 22,880 fathoms (twenty-six miles or 41.83 km) of hemp was used for the standing and running rigging. While some was grown in England, most of the raw hemp was imported from the Baltic.

13. How many pulley blocks were used for her rigging?

Approximately 768, the largest being 26 inches long, the smallest 6 inches. Additional blocks were used for a variety of functions throughout the ship: anchors and their associated gear, ship's boats and storing ship. Besides spares, a further 628 blocks were used to work the guns.

14. How & where were her sails made?

The sails were made from flax woven into long canvas strips called bolts. A bolt of canvas was thirty-nine yards long and two feet in width. Most of the canvas supplied to the Royal Navy was manufactured in mills in Dundee, Scotland, Northern Ireland and Dorset. Finished bolts of canvas were purchased by the government and sent to the royal dockyards for conversion into sails. The sails for *Victory* were made up in the sail loft at Chatham Dockyard. All sails were sewn by hand. It took twenty men eighty-three

Mizzen mast & mizzen topsail bits on the poop deck   Photograph by P Goodwin days to make a suit of sails for a first rate ship. This work required 64,000 yards (58,240 metres) of seaming to make one set of sails. Each man would thus have to produce 3,200 yards (2,926 metres) of stitching to complete the work. To identify naval sails, a thin blue wavy line was painted down the centre of each bolt. Today this line is automatically woven into the cloth. To identify individual sails within the sail rooms, each sail had a marked wooden tally attached to it.

15. How much sail did Victory carry?

The maximum number of sails that could be set was thirty-seven, including her staysails and studding sails. This vast amount of canvas gave her a sail area of 6,510 square yards (5,468.4 square metres) - a third larger than a football pitch. However, it was unlikely that all her sails were set at the same time. According to the boatswain's store muster for March 1805 a total of fifty-nine sails (including spares) was carried on the ship. The original fore topsail used at Trafalgar still exists and is currently undergoing restoration.

16. How much did it cost to build Victory?

At the time of her launch in 1765, *Victory* cost £63,176 (over £50 million today). The Royal Navy's next generation of aircraft carriers will cost over two billion pounds each.

The 74 gun ship HMS Hastings laying in ordinary in the Medway   Illustration by E W Cooke

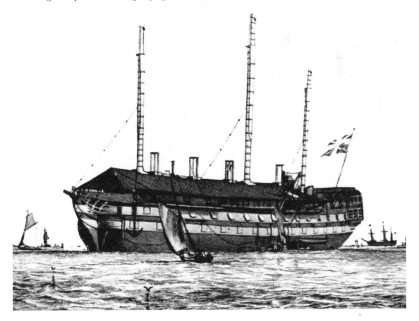

Estimated sizes & area of one suit of thirty-seven sails for the Victory

Name of Sail	Head ft	Foot ft	Leach ft	Luff ft	Depth ft	Area sq ft	Area sq yds
Sprit topsail	37	56	33		32	1,488.0	165.33
Spritsail	56	56	27		27	1,512.0	168.00
Fore course	88	84	46		46	3,956.0	439.55
Fore topsail	54	80	52		49	3,283.0	364.77
Fore topgallant	34	58	33		31	1,426.0	158.40
Fore royal	21	33			12	318.0	35.33
Main course	85	92	40		47	4,159.5	462.16
Main topsail	56	84	57		54	3,780.0	420.00
Main topgallant	36	56	37		35	1,435.0	159.44
Main royal	24	38			17	527.0	58.55
Mizzen topsail	40	60	45		42	2,100.0	233.33
Mizzen topgallant	27	41	28		26	884.0	98.20
Mizzen royal	15	26			10	205.0	22.70
Mizzen (driver)	55	70	69	28		2,618.0	290.88
Fore lower stunsail (2)	35	35	41	41	41	2,870.0	318.88
Fore tops'l stunsail (2)	24	32	54	51	40	2,240.0	248.88
Fore t'gllnt stunsail (2)	15	23	35	32	31	1,178.0	138.88
Main lower stunsail (2)	36	36	50	50	50	3,600.0	400.00
Main tops'l stunsail (2)	26	36	62	58	54	3,348.0	372.00
Main t'gllnt stunsail (2)	18	29	40	36	36	2,340.0	260.00
Flying jib	50		54	60		1,350.0	150.00
Jib	50		78	85		1,950.0	216.66
Fore topmast staysail	49		73	84		1,788.5	198.72
Fore staysail	43		46	54		989.0	109.88
Main staysail	57		43	70		1,225.5	136.16
Main topmast staysail	58		78	66		2,262.0	251.33
Middle staysail	48	45	39	23		1,395.0	155.00
Main t'gllnt staysail	47	40	42	20		1,240.0	137.77
Mizzen staysail	44	40	21	38		1,180.0	131.11
Mizn topmast staysail	47	38	20	50		1,330.0	147.77
Mizzen t'gllnt staysail	39	29	8	34		609.0	67.66

Data compiled by Peter Goodwin from scale drawings by J McKay

Fore lower shrouds, deadeyes, lashed anchor buoys & starboard fish davit stowed on deck

Photograph by P Goodwin

17. When was Victory launched?

Victory was 'floated out of the dock' on 7 May 1765. She was not launched as we know it because large ships such as this were built in a dry dock on level keel blocks, as opposed to a slipway running into the water.

18. When & why was it decided to name her Victory?

When building commenced the ship had not been given a name. Although the name *Victory* seemed suitable, there were some doubts as the previous *Victory* was wrecked with all hands lost. Finally, in a letter from the Admiralty Board dated 30 October 1760, it was directed that the ship was to be named *Victory*. The choice of name had been strongly influenced by Britain's successes against her enemies during the previous year 1759, which became known as *annus mirabilis* or 'marvellous year'. It was also the turning point of the Seven Years' War.

19. What purpose did Victory serve, once fitted out?

None. The Seven Years' War ended two years before she was completed. The ship was therefore laid up 'in ordinary' and maintained in preparation for future wars. She remained at her moorings for thirteen years.

Curator's view from the truck of the main topgallant mast - 180 feet (54.86 m) above the deck
Photograph by P Goodwin

Dignitaries visit Victory circa 1936   By kind permission of the Commanding Officer HMS *Victory*

Facts about Victory

20. When did Victory first sail on active service?

Victory was first commissioned in February 1778 under the flag of Admiral Augustus Keppel. Subsequently the ship was fitted out for sea at a cost of £13,296. As flagship of the Grand Fleet, *Victory* sailed from Portsmouth and was first in action against the French fleet commanded by Admiral d'Orvilliers off Ushant on 27 July 1778. This battle was indecisive.

21. Victory was flagship to which famous admirals?

> Augustus Keppel - 1778
> Sir Hyde Parker - 1781
> Richard Kempenfelt - 1782
> Lord Richard Howe - 1782 and again from 1789 to 1790
> Lord Samuel Hood - 1790 to 1794
> Sir John Jervis - 1795 to 1797
> Lord Horatio Nelson - 1803 to 1805
> Sir James Saumarez - 1808 to 1812

Lord Augustus Keppel[8]   Sir Hyde Parker

22. How fast could *Victory* sail & how close to the wind could she steer?

Under ideal sailing conditions she could make between eight and nine knots (approximately 10 mph or 16 kmh). She could run before the wind as fast as ten to eleven knots and was said to 'forereach upon most, or all ships of three decks we have been in company with'.[9] The closest she could steer was between six and a half and seven points (73 to 78 degrees off the wind).

23. Was there ever a mutiny on board *Victory*?

None discovered. During the mutinies of 1797, *Victory* served in the Mediterranean under Admiral Sir John Jervis. She had just been engaged at

Richard Kempenfelt   Lord Richard Howe

Lord Samuel Hood

Sir John Jervis, Earl of St Vincent

the successful battle of Cape St Vincent, consequently morale and discipline within the Mediterranean fleet were high irrespective of the problems at home.

24. Was Victory ever seriously damaged during her active career?

The most serious damage *Victory* sustained was at the battle of Trafalgar where she lost her fore topmasts and yards, studdingsail booms and yards, jibbooms and her entire mizzen mast. In addition, her hull was much damaged from gun shot and about two hundred hand grenades thrown onto her decks. Fires started on the boat booms and near the after hanging magazine,

Lord Horatio Nelson

Sir James Samaurez

Trafalgar Day, 21 October 1911: 'Lord Nelson's Own' Troop (8th Portsmouth) visited HMS Victory to do homage to the memory of the hero of Trafalgar. The scouts formed a hollow square around the spot where Nelson fell, and the troop chaplin gave them an address. A message from the present Earl Nelson was read: 'Our great admiral gave himself to do his duty to his king and country, and ever thought of them before himself. Learn, therefore, in everything to be able to help others, and be always watchful for opportunities of doing so.' By kind permission of the Commanding Officer HMS Victory

but were quickly extinguished. Most of the boats stowed on the ship were stove in and her starboard side suffered severely with many gunport lids lost and both anchors shot away. After the battle the starboard side of her forecastle had to be shored up and she was making twelve inches (30 cms) of water an hour in the hold from shot holes below the waterline. The flat beakhead bulkhead, a transverse partition at the fore end of the ship, was riddled with holes made by both gun and grape shot. Over 200 panes of glass in the stern were shattered and the cupids on the figurehead lost either an arm or a leg. After the battle she was towed to Gibraltar by *Neptune*.

25. What was Victory's longest voyage?

The longest time *Victory* spent at sea was under the command of Lord Nelson. She sailed from Spithead on 20 May 1803 and returned on 18 August 1805 without entering port, a period of two years and three months. Within a month she sailed for Trafalgar.

Rose Lashing

Ship's wheel, binnacle, log line & the officer of the watch's slate bearing Nelson's famous signal &
signal number sixteen, 'close action'   Photograph by P Goodwin

Sailors & marines compete at gun drill   By kind permission of the Commanding Officer HMS *Victory*

Victory's armament

26. What was Victory's armament when commissioned?

Lower gun deck	thirty	42 pounders[10]
Middle gun deck	twenty-eight	24 pounders
Upper gun deck	thirty	12 pounders
Quarter deck	ten	6 pounders
Forecastle	two	6 pounders

27. What was her armament at Trafalgar?

Lower gun deck	thirty	32 pounders
Middle gun deck	twenty-eight	24 pounders
Upper gun deck	thirty	long 12 pounders
Quarter deck	twelve	short 12 pounders
Forecastle	two	medium 12 pounders
	two	68 pdr carronades
Other	one	18 pdr carronade (used in launch)

28. What is a '24 pounder'?

Twenty-four pounds (10.9kg) is the weight of the solid round shot (cannon ball) that a gun of this classification fired.

29. How much gunpowder was used to fire a 24 lb shot?

Range	Proportion to shot	Charge
Extreme	one third weight of shot	8.0 lbs (3.63 kg)
Point blank	one quarter weight of shot	6.0 lbs (2.72 kg)
Reduced	one fifth weight of shot	4.8 lbs (2.20 kg)

To distinguish the charge size for each range, cartridges were marked with the charge weight in painted numerals, the colours being black (extreme), blue (point blank) and red (reduced). While charges for other sized cannon differed, the colour coding remained identical.

30. What is a carronade?

A carronade is a short lightweight gun that fired a heavy shot at a low velocity over a short range. The internal bore of this type of gun was chambered so that less gunpowder was used in proportion to the shot fired. Unlike standard ship's guns, the carronade was mounted on a carriage fitted with a sliding block to take the recoil. Another advantage over the standard gun was that the carriage was fitted with transverse castors which permitted the gun to be trained over a greater angle of fire. In effect the carronade was a 'heavier and more powerful' naval version of the military howitzer. Because of its destructive power at close range, it was known by British sailors as a 'smasher' and by her enemies as a 'devil gun'.

Gun drill circa 1900   By kind permission of the Commanding Officer HMS *Victory*

31. Why is it called a carronade?

The name is taken from the Carron Iron Company situated on the river Carron near Falkirk in Stirlingshire, Scotland, where the gun was originally developed. The carronade was jointly invented by General Robert Melville, an experienced military officer and Charles Gasgoigne, the gunfounder and partner of the Carron Iron Company. The carronade was first manufactured in 1778 and officially introduced into the navy in 1779.

32. What was the weight & range of Victory's guns?

Gun type	Weight cwt/tons	Weight tonnes
32 pdr	55 cwt (2.75 t)	2.79
24 pdr	50 cwt (2.50 t)	2.54
12 pdr long	34 cwt (1.70 t)	1.72
12 pdr medium	32 cwt (1.60 t)	1.63
12 pdr short	31 cwt (1.40 t)	1.57
68 pdr carronade	35 cwt (1.75 t)	1.78
18 pdr carronade	10 cwt (0.50 t)	1.51

Gun Type	Point Blank Range			Maximum Range		
	yds	miles	km	yds	miles	km
32 pdr	400	0.23	0.37	2,640	1.5	2.40
24 pdr	400	0.23	0.37	1,980	1.125	1.80
12 pdr	375	0.21	0.34	1,320	0.750	1.20
68 pdr carronade	450	0.26	0.42	1,280	0.730	1.17
18 pdr carronade	270	0.15	0.24	1,000	0.570	1.91

Carriage mounted 12 pounder carronade

Illustration by E W Cooke

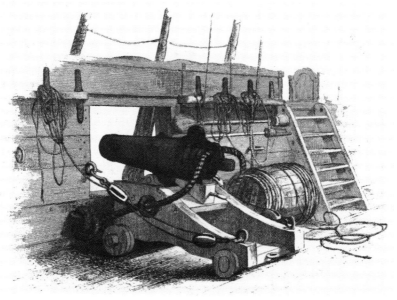

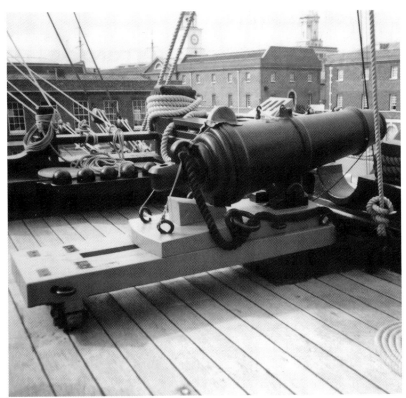

Victory's starboard 68 pounder carronade on a slide carriage   Photograph by P Goodwin

For standard guns, maximum range is given with guns elevated at ten degrees, an angle rarely used at sea. With carronades, maximum range is given with guns elevated at five degrees, an angle that could be set at sea.

33. What was the total weight of shot discharged in a single broadside?

Her broadside weight was 1,148 lbs (522 kg). When *Victory* first opened fire at the battle of Trafalgar all the guns, with the exception of the carronades on the larboard[11] side were treble-shotted. This gave her an opening broadside weight of 3,240 lbs (1,473 kg) - nearly 1.5 tons (1.6 tonnes) of iron. This mass of iron left the ship at a velocity of approximately 1,600 feet (487.7 m) *per* second.

34. How much gunpowder was used on Victory at Trafalgar?

The total amount of gunpowder used for cartridges during the battle was 17,100 lbs or a little over 7.625 tons (7.8 tonnes).

The grand staircase, removed in 1923   By kind permission of the Commanding Officer HMS *Victory*

35. How much shot was fired from her guns at Trafalgar?

The number and weight of round shot used were as follows:

Size	Rounds	Pounds	Tons	Tonnes
32 lb	997	31,904	14.24	14.46
24 lb	872	20,928	9.34	9.49
12 lb	800	9,600	4.29	4.36
Total	2,669	62,432	27.87	28.32

Additional types of shot expended during the battle were:

Size	Double-Headed	Grape	Pounds	Tons	Tonnes
32 lb	10	10	640	.29	.29
24 lb	11	20	744	.33	.34
12 lb	14	156	2,040	.91	.92
Total	35	186	3,424	1.53	1.55

Cross section of 32 pounder

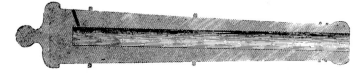

'Saluting the quarter deck' circa 1930   By kind permission of the Commanding Officer HMS *Victory*

The headrails & brackets of Victory's bow

Photograph by P Goodwin

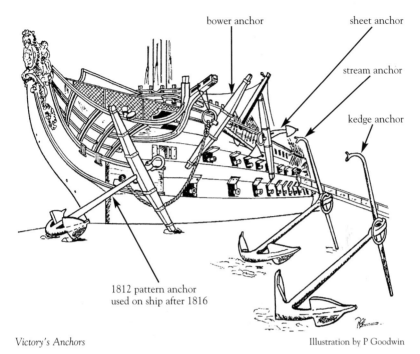

bower anchor

sheet anchor

stream anchor

kedge anchor

1812 pattern anchor
used on ship after 1816

Victory's Anchors   Illustration by P Goodwin

Victory's stores & equipment

36. How many anchors did Victory carry?

Victory carried seven anchors:

No	Type	tons	cwt	qtr	lbs	tonnes
1	Best bower anchor	4	9	1	14	4.54
1	Small bower anchor	4	8	2	22	4.51
2	Sheet anchors	4	4	3	12	4.31
1	Stream anchor	1	1	3	7	1.10
1	Large kedge anchor	-	10	0	7	0.51
1	Small kedge anchor	-	5	3	7	0.30

The best bower anchor served as one of the two main anchors used for holding the ship in deep water and bower. Being the heaviest and strongest anchor it was always rigged to the starboard bow (hence the name 'bower') of the ship.

The small bower anchor, secured on the larboard bow, served the same purpose as the best bower though not as strong.

Sheet anchors, one on each side, served as spares for the bowers should their cables part in heavy weather, or the anchors are lost.

35

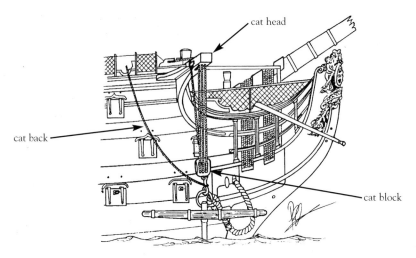

'Catting' Victory's anchor   Illustration by P Goodwin

The stream anchor was a lightweight anchor used for anchoring the ship in low tide streams and shallow waters and could be used for warping the ship. It was normally stored lashed to the starboard sheet anchor.

Kedge anchors were used to keep a ship steady and clear of her bower anchor when riding in harbour and also used to 'kedge' or warp the ship. Kedging or warping means to haul the ship along by bringing in her cable. The kedge anchor was then taken by boat and re-laid, then hauling was repeated. This was done in confined waters or when there was no wind.

'Fishing' Victory's anchor   Illustration by P Goodwin

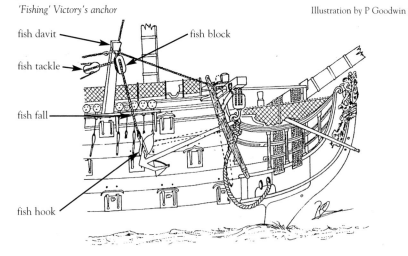

Larboard bower anchor hanging from the cathead, fish davit to right   Photograph by P Goodwin

37. How many anchor cables did Victory carry?

Victory carried fifteen cables:

Type/Use	No	Circumference		Diameter	
		in	cm	in	cm
Cable	6	24	60.96	7 fi	19.7
Cable	1	23	58.42	7/	18.4
Cable	1	16	40.64	5	12.7
Cable	4	9	22.86	2 7/8	7.3
Cable	1	7 fi	19.05	2 3/8	6.0
Cable	1	7	17.78	2/	5.7
Messenger	1	16	40.64	5	12.7
Messenger	1	14	35.56	4 fi	11.4

'Nipping' Victory's anchor cable to the smaller messenger cable   Illustration by P Goodwin

Anchor cable turned up on the riding bitts & messenger rope   Photograph by P Goodwin

Anchoring a square rigged ship:

Before anchoring, the cable was brought up from the cable tier and flaked out in long lengths along the gun deck, its outer end was hove out of the hawse hole and bent to the anchor ring. The anchor was then unhitched from its sea-stowed position. When ready to anchor the ship, the following ship-wide operations were carried out:

A. The helm was put over to steer the ship into the wind. On most occasions all smaller sails were taken in to reduce speed.

B. As the ship turned head-on into the wind, the wind effect on the sails set the sail 'aback' bringing the ship to a standstill. Final soundings were taken of water depth to determine how much cable was to paid out.

C. Once the ship had stopped in the water the anchor was let go from the cathead.

D. With the sails set aback, the ship then started to make sternboard that is, to sail backwards. As it did so, the anchor made fast into the sea bed and the cable was paid out as required. Once run out, the ship was stopped by taking in all sail.

The end of the cable inside the ship was turned up on huge timber beams called riding bitts and secured with rope cable stoppers. These bitts took the strain of the ship as she was 'riding on her anchor'.

Illustration by P Goodwin

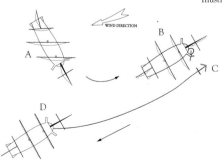

38. How many boats did Victory carry?

Victory carried six boats at the time of Trafalgar:

Type	Length	Use
Launch	34ft (10.36m)	Storing and watering ship; anchor work; taking assault parties ashore; general work boat.
Barge	32ft (9.75m)	For conveying the admiral to and from the ship.
Pinnace	28ft (8.54m)	For conveying the officers and general use.
Cutter (two)	25ft (7.62m)	Sea boats for conveying personnel from ship to ship; inshore survey work and general use.
Cutter	18ft (5.48m)	A second sea boat.

Victory's boats stowed in the waist: left to right, admiral's barge, pinnace & launch with an eighteen foot cutter stored inside   By kind permission of the Commanding Officer HMS Victory

One of the ships twenty-five foot cutters & starboard best bower anchor   Photograph by P Goodwin

39. Where were boats stowed & what happened to them in battle?

Four boats were housed on skid beams fitted across the waist of the ship, an open space between the quarterdeck and forecastle. The other two boats were generally slung on one of the two sets of davits fitted either side of the poop deck. According to Midshipman Rivers' journal and the carpenter's expenses (both held in the Royal Naval Museum), when *Victory* went into battle at Trafalgar most of the boats remained on the skid beams.[12] The sea boats, hanging on the davits, were lowered and towed astern. Rarely would all boats be lowered before battle, owing to the time required to remove them from the ship.

40. How were boats swung over the ship's side?

Those slung on davits were simply lowered on the fall tackle, rove through sheaves at the ends of the davits, the davits being lowered first to a horizontal position to clear the boat from the ship's side. Swinging out the other larger boats housed on the skid beams was more difficult. In short, the operation required the boat to be moved both vertically and horizontally. These two operations were usually done at the same time. All the ropes used to move the boat were secured to lifting eyes inside the boat. Vertical hoist for taking the boat off the skid beams was achieved by using tackle secured to the burton pendants suspended from the heads of the fore and main masts. To move the boat horizontally, tackle, rigged to the yardarms of the fore and main lower yards, served like cranes. For both safety and ease, the operation was assisted by the use of the fore or 'jeer' capstan. Once all four tackles were secured it was simply a question of hoisting and pulling the appropriate ropes to swing the boat out over the ship's side. Once in this position, the tackle leading from both mast heads was disengaged, leaving the boat free to be lowered into the sea using the tackle rigged to the yards. Recovering the boat was simply a reverse process.

41. What stores & provisions did Victory carry?

Item	Tons	Tonnes
Gunpowder	35	35.60
Shot	120	121.90
Coal	50	50.80
Beef and pork	30	30.50
Bread or biscuit	45	45.70
Butter	2	2.03
Flour	10	10.16
Peas	15	15.25
Beer	50	50.80
Water	300	304.80
Sand, pitch, tar, etc	20	20.30
Ballast[13]	210	213.36
Total[14]	887	901.24

42. What other stores were carried?

Specialist stores and equipment were held by the boatswain, gunner and the carpenter. The boatswain's stores comprised all gear associated with the ship's rigging: cables, rope, blocks, sails, tar, pitch and tallow. He also carried the necessary items required for the ship's cleanliness: deck scrubbers, brushes and swabs (mops). The gunner carried equipment relating to the guns and powder rooms: rammers, sponges, wadhooks, cartridges, copper powder scoops, gunlocks, flints and powder horns. He was also responsible for all small arms: pikes, muskets, pistols, hatchets, cutlasses, bayonets, musket and pistol shot. The carpenter's stores comprised bolts, nails, fastenings, paint, iron plate, lanterns, locks, hasps, tools such as adzes, planes, saws and pin mauls, etc. He also had caulking tools, ladles, pitch pots, stoves and glass, and carried timber and planks for carrying out repairs at sea.

43. How many small arms & weapons were carried?

According to an 1805 muster, the gunner held the following:

Muskets[15]	142		Pistols (pairs)	70
Bayonets	142		Grenades	200
Cutlasses	187		Halberds	1
Pikes	100		Drum	1

Museum on the middle gun deck in Victory circa 1907. Although many of the artefacts had doubtful provenance, the museum did exhibit Victory's original fore & main topsails used at the battle of Trafalgar. While the fore topsail still exists, the main topsail disappeared during World War II

By kind permission of the Commanding Officer HMS *Victory*

A marine private guarding the spirit room
Illustration by Colonel Cyril Field, courtesy of the Royal Marines Museum

Victory's crew

44. What was Victory's complement?

Her full complement was 850, but at Trafalgar it was only 820:[16]

Commissioned officers	No	Petty officers	No
Captain	1	Master's mates	6
First lieutenant	1	Boatswain's mates	4
Lieutenants	8	Gunner's mates	4
Captain of marines	1	Quarter gunners	13
Lieutenants of marines	2	Carpenter's mates	4
Second lieutenant of marines	1	Carpenter's crew	10
Total	14	Quartermasters	9
		Quartermaster's mates	4
Warrant officers	No	Armourer's mates	2
Master	1	Gunsmith	1
Boatswain	1	Master at arms	1
Gunner	1	Sailmaker	1
Carpenter	1	Sailmaker's mate	1
Surgeon	1	Cook	1
Purser	1	Ropemaker	1
Chaplain	1	Coxswain	1
Armourer	1	Yeoman of the sheets	3
Midshipmen	21	Yeoman of the powder room	2
Total	29	Caulker	1
		Caulker's mate	1
		Total	70

Seamen & Marines	No		Supply, secretariat & retinue	No
Able Seamen	212		Agent victualler's clerk	1
Ordinary Seamen	193		Purser's steward	1
Landsmen	87		Supply	29
Boys	31		Admiral's secretary	1
Marines	142		Secretary's clerk	1
Total	665		Captain's clerk	1
			Retinue (valets & servants)	5
			Surgeon's mates	2
			Sailmaker's crew	1
			Total	42

Signal flag lockers at the after end of the poop deck

Photograph by P Goodwin

Warrant officer & seamen on poop deck By kind permission of the Commanding Officer HMS *Victory*

45. How much was a captain paid in 1805?

A captain's pay varied according to the size of the ship he commanded and his seniority. A captain of a first rate ship of 100 guns received twice as much as the captain of a 6th rate ship of 20 guns. The pay for a captain of *Victory* was approximately £30 to £32 a month.

46. Who was the master of Victory at Trafalgar?

The master and senior warrant officer, was Thomas Atkinson. His main tasks concerned the safe navigation and pilotage of the ship and keeping the ship's official logbook. He was also responsible for sails and rigging, anchors and stowage of stores in the ship's hold. The way the ship was stored was important as it effected the ship's trim and sailing abilities. His other duties related to the issue of beer and spirits. To assist him he had master's mates, quartermasters and quartermaster's mates. Thomas Atkinson died in 1836 and was buried in St Andrew's churchyard at Farlington, near Portsmouth.

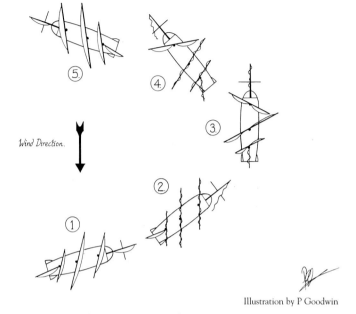

Wind Direction.

Illustration by P Goodwin

Tacking ship

This manœuvre involved turning the head of the ship through the wind. This was undertaken as follows. The diagram shows the ship close hauled on a larboard tack - the wind coming from the larboard side:

1. **'Stations for stays'**. This order alerts the crew to man their respective stations and prepare the braces for running. The helm was eased to leeward (downwind) to increase the speed of the ship. Once ready the next order **'Stand by to tack, ready about'** is given.

2. **'Helm's a'lee'**. The jib sails are eased to assist the turn and because wind is spilled from the square sails, the wind effect driving the ship is reduced.

3. **'Haul taut, main and mizzen sail haul'**. The yards on the main and mizzen masts are braced around quickly to the opposite side catching some wind to drive the stem backwards (stern-board). The rudder is centred once the ship slows down (loses way). The wind sets the fore mast sails 'aback' pushing the head of the ship through the wind.

4. The boom of the mizzen sail or spanker is eased over to larboard, likewise the sheet of the jib, in preparation for a starboard tack. **'Let go and haul'**. The fore mast yards are immediately braced round. The wind fills the sails on all three masts, mizzen sail and jib bringing the ship onto a starboard tack. All ropes are coiled or secured.

Wearing ship

This manœuvre involved turning the stem of the ship through the wind. This was undertaken as follows. The diagram shows the ship close hauled on a larboard tack - the wind coming from the larboard side.

1. *'Stations for wearing ship'*. The crew to man their respective stations and prepare the braces for running. Once ready the next order, *'Stand by to wear ship'* is given.
2. *'Up mainsail and mizzen (spanker), Brace in the after yards'*. The main course and mizzen sail are brailed up to prevent them opposing the turn. *'Up Helm'*, the rudder turns the ship to starboard taking the ship's stern across the wind.
3. *'Main and Mizzen mast, let go and haul'*. The yards of the main and mizzen masts are braced round to feather the sails allowing the wind to spill from the sails.
4. As the wind comes onto the starboard quarter acting on the sails of the fore mast and the headsail (jibs), the ship begins to turn.
5. *'Square the fore sails, let go and haul'*. The fore yards are squared and the headsails are hauled over to larboard.
6. *'Haul aboard, haul out'*. The mainsail and mizzen sail (spanker) are re-set and the lee braces of the fore yards are braced round.
7. With the sails on the main and mizzen masts filling, the ship gathers speed.
8. The ship now proceeds on a starboard tack. All sails are trimmed and respective ropes coiled or secured.

Illustration by P Goodwin

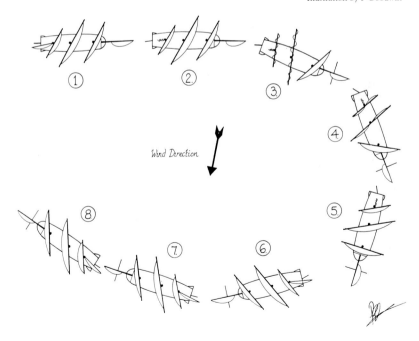

47. What are midshipmen?

The 'young gentlemen' usually came from professional families and were sent to sea to train as naval officers. Like Nelson, most entered service at twelve or thirteen. They learned the skills of able seamen. Having 'learnt the ropes', their training became more professional, learning navigation and seamanship under the guidance of the master, and mathematics, algebra and trigonometry from the schoolmaster or chaplain. On duty they would assist the officer of the watch, taking charge of the log line, the ship's boat and in battle take charge of groups of guns. When they first entered the ship they lived in the gunroom. When a little older they shifted to the midshipmen's berth in the cockpit on the orlop deck. Some midshipmen were promoted from the lower deck and were invariable older men.

48. What is a warrant officer?

A warrant officer had a crucial trade or skill. They were appointed before commissioned officers and their service tended to be more continuous. Pursers, gunners, boatswains and carpenters were warranted by the Admiralty and appointed by the Navy Board; masters, surgeons and cooks were appointed by Navy Board warrants.

49. Who were the oldest & youngest members of the crew?

The oldest man on board in 1805 was the purser, Walter Burke, who was sixty-seven. Aged twelve, the youngest was Tom Twitchet.

'Anchors, &c.'   Illustration by E W Cooke

Learning the ropes

50. What was a purser?

The purser acted as the ship's grocer. He took delivery of all foodstuffs, provisions, beer and spirits from the victualling yards. He purchased provisions and supplies in foreign ports. He issued hammocks and bedding, and sold slops and tobacco to the seamen. As smoking was restricted, most men chewed their tobacco. Everything issued was carefully registered against each man's name, to ensure deductions were made from their pay. On a ship like *Victory* the purser paid a bond of £1,200. To obtain a return on this investment he made a profit on items sold and deducted a 'purser's eighth' on dry provisions and a 'purser's quart' on beer. To prevent embezzlement his ledgers were inspected by the captain each month. Moreover, a purser could not get another position until his accounts were approved.

Captain Hardy's day cabin looking larboard   Photograph by P Goodwin

51. What was a powder monkey?

A powder monkey was the term given to any personnel who passed filled cartridges and shot during action from the magazines below decks. The suggestion that this work was done entirely by ship's boys is a myth. Eighty to ninety people were needed to perform this task in battle and there were only thirty-one boys on *Victory*. As the ship's boys ranged in age from twelve to nineteen, many of them were not really boys. It would also be absurd to suggest that powder monkeys spent the entire battle running to and from the magazines in the lower regions of the ship to the various decks above. This was not only impractical, but physically impossible. Recent research into standing orders of ships of the period reveals that boys were not allowed in the magazines.[17]

For efficiency and to ensure a continuous supply of powder, teams of men, older boys and women (when carried on board) were organised on each deck to relay cartridges in a continuous chain between the powder magazines and the appropriate gundecks, with some men stationed at hatchways to hand cartridges up to the next deck. Younger boys were used on the gundecks to convey powder from hatchways to the guns and to douse down loose powder around the guns to prevent explosions. In most cases, the ship would be fighting on one side only - leaving the deck on the opposite side relatively free for the powder monkeys to run back and forth from the hatches to replenish the salt boxes placed well behind the guns. Each salt box, containing two ready charges, was the responsibility of a member of the gun crew designated the powder man.

For better organisation and to avoid confusion of powder charge sizes, guns were supplied from individual magazines:[18]

Gun location	Type	Magazine
Quarter deck	12 pdr	After hanging magazine
Forecastle	12 pdr	After hanging magazine
Forecastle	68 pdr carronade	Grand magazine
Upper gun deck	12 pdr	After hanging magazine
Middle gun deck	24 pdr	Fore hanging magazine
Lower gun deck	32 pdr	Grand magazine

52. How much were seamen paid in 1805?

After the increase in 1797 (their first increase for 144 years), able seamen earned a shilling a day (approximately £1.50 a month). As they were victualled (although their families were not) they earned slightly more than agricultural labourers (£1.50 a month) and urban unskilled labourers (£1.80 a month). However, compared with shipwrights (£3.12 a month plus lodgings) and fine mule spinners (£7.50 a month), they remained poorly paid.

Seamen's hammocks, set sixteen inches apart, on the lower gun deck   Photograph by P Goodwin

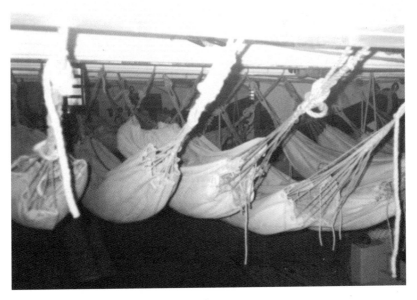

This was a key reason why merchant seamen (who in wartime could earn as much as £6 a month plus victuals) were anxious to avoid impressment and why naval seamen valued prize money.[19]

53. What was prize money?

When an enemy ship had been captured it was handed over as a 'prize' to the Admiralty who would then decide the entire value of the vessel including its contents. Once evaluated, a sum of money called 'prize money' was distributed between all members of the crew of the ship that had captured the vessel. The distribution of money was not equal, but proportional to the rank and status of each person. The share received by the common seamen was very small. Only one eighth of the entire sum was shared evenly between those who were below the rank of petty officer, which comprised about seventy-five *per cent* of the ship's complement.

Galley flue, steam gratings & belfrey on the forecastle   Photograph by P Goodwin

Left: Water and provisions casks, iron & shingle ballast in the hold
Right: Elm tree pump (bored out from a single elm tree) took direct suction from the sea to supply water for washing decks & fighting fires　　　　　　　　　　　　　Photographs by P Goodwin

Government grant and prize money given to *Victory*'s crew after Trafalgar:

Class	Ranks	Government grant	Prize money
1st	Captain	£2,389　7s 6d	£973　0s 0d
2nd	Commissioned officers & marine captain	£161　0s 0d	£65 11s 0d
3rd	Non-commissioned & warrant officers Marine lieutenants	£108 12s 0d	£44　4s 6d
4th	Mates, coxswain, midshipmen, marine sergeants	£26　6s 0d	£10　4s 0d
5th	Able & ordinary seamen, landsmen Marine privates, miscellaneous supply, boys	£4 12s 6d	£1 17s 6d

54. What other tradesmen & specialists were on board?

In addition to being the eighteenth century's most complicated piece of machinery, a ship was like a small town or a microcosm of society. It needed many trades to support daily life on board. For this, *Victory* carried the following personnel:

Sailmaker and his mates　　　　Carpenter's mates
Ropemaker　　　　　　　　　　Gunsmith
Armourer and his mates　　　　Cooper
Poulterer　　　　　　　　　　　Victuallers
Stewards and servants

There were also specialist seamen such as:
> Boatswain's mates
> Quartermaster and his mates
> Gunner's mates and quarter gunners
> Captains of the forecastle, foretop and maintop
> Yeomen of the sheets
> Yeomen of the powder room
> Master-at-arms and two ship's corporals

55. What were the gunner's duties?

The gunner, William Rivers, was responsible for the maintenance of all guns, carriages, associated equipment and side arms: rammers, wadhooks, sponges, vent prickers, vent reamers and gunlocks. He ensured that gunpowder kept in the magazine was safe and dry, and that there was a plentiful supply of ready-use cartridges available. Assisting him were six mates, twelve quarter gunners and two yeoman of the powder room. He was also responsible for all small arms: muskets, bayonets, pistols, cutlasses, pikes and hatchets. For this equipment he had an armourer, his mates and a gunsmith. The gunner was also in charge of the gunroom situated at the after end of the lower gun deck where he kept a watch over the ship's boys.[20]

Marines' hammocks & mess tables on the middle gun deck   Photograph by P Goodwin

Captain Adair's epaulette & the bar shot that killed eight marines on the poop deck
Illustration by C Field, Courtesy of the Royal Marines Museum

56. How many marines were on Victory?

The company from the Chatham Division included 146 officers and men:

Rank & File	No
Captain of marines (Charles Adair)	1
Lieutenants	2
Second lieutenants	1
Sergeants	4
Corporals	3
Privates	132
Drummer	2
Trumpeter	1
Total	146

57. What were the marines' duties?

Marines served as a professional military unit, both afloat and ashore. They also protected the ship's officers from the crew. During battle they provided extra manpower to operate guns, small arms fire and disciplined defence at close quarters. They participated in attacks on coastal installations and cutting-out (capturing) enemy ships at anchor. Under normal sailing conditions they were employed as sentinels guarding the powder rooms, magazines, the spirit room and other storerooms, and the entrances to the admiral's and officers' quarters. This precaution was considered essential after the mutinies in 1797. Their other duties were to give general assistance to seamen when unskilled heavy labour was required, such as hauling on ropes when the ship was manoeuvring. They also supplied manpower to help turn the capstan to weigh anchor or embark heavy stores.

Victory's Trafalgar crew origins

English	515	German	2
Irish	88	Indian	2
Scottish	67	Italian	9
Welsh	30	Jamaican	1
African	1	Maltese	6
American	22	Norwegian	2
Brazilian	1	Portuguese	1
Canadian	2	Swedish	4
Danish	2	Swiss	2
Dutch	7	West Indian	4
French	4	Unrecorded	48
		Total	820

Figurehead: *Victory's figurehead is a faithful representation of that fitted at the battle of Trafalgar which replaced the elaborate original during the 'large repair' of 1801-1803.*[21] *The design comprises two cupids supporting the royal coat of arms surmounted with the royal crown. The arms bear the Latin inscription of the Order of the Garter:* Honi Soit Qui Mal Y Pense *(Shame to him who evil thinks). At the time the royal coat of arms included the escutcheon of Hanover - the white horse and Hanoverian crown at the centre. Each cupid wears a coloured sash: starboard, blue; larboard, red - suggesting these figures may represent cherubim and seraphim. The figurehead was carved by George Williams for a cost of £50. We know from Midshipman Rivers' account of the battle of Trafalgar that the starboard figure had its leg shot away, and the larboard figure its arm.*[22]

By kind permission of the Commanding Officer HMS *Victory*

Victory flying Nelson's signal for the centenary of the battle of Trafalgar, 21 October 1905
By kind permission of the Commanding Officer HMS *Victory*

Life on board Victory

58. How were seamen organised & how many hours did they work?

The seamen were divided into two watches: Starboard and Larboard working every other watch during the working day, which started at noon:

Watch Name	Start	Finish	Duration	Watch
Afternoon	12.00 pm	4.00 pm	4 hrs	Starboard
First dog	4.00 pm	6.00 pm	2 hrs	Larboard
Last dog	6.00 pm	8.00 pm	2 hrs	Starboard
First	8.00 pm	12.00 am	4 hrs	Larboard
Middle	12.00 am	4.00 am	4 hrs	Starboard
Morning	4.00 am	8.00 am	4 hrs	Larboard
Forenoon	8.00 am	12.00 pm	4 hrs	Starboard

The starboard watch worked fourteen hours and the larboard watch ten. These hours were reversed the following day because of the two short two-hour dog watches. When manœuvring ship, tacking or wearing, both watches would be deployed, irrespective of the time of day or night. In any emergency situation or heavy weather it was common to 'call all hands' from below to attend the ship and sails. For efficiency each of the two watches, starboard and larboard, were subdivided into two parts, first and second part

Gratings set up for a flogging at the break of the quarter deck   Photograph by P Goodwin

of starboard, in order to split the work load when sailing was easy. This permitted one half of the watch to attend to other duties or train at the guns. In addition to standard watch-keeping duties, all hands 'turned to' during the forenoon, cleaning, repairing at their appropriate 'parts of ship'. In the early evening and sometimes during the forenoon, they were exercised at gun drill to ensure battle readiness.

59. Why was strict discipline essential at sea?

Discipline, not to be confused with punishment, was essential to the management of a ship at sea where lives frequently depended on each member of the crew understanding their rôles and following orders under all conditions. A fighting ship served to protect trade, to fight and defeat England's enemies. Even without the prospect of battle the sea is a hostile environment where failure to observe, or to respond swiftly to an arising or emergency situation could lead to disaster. The rules of discipline which governed the whole crew were contained in the Articles of War revised in 1749. By custom and order thirty-six articles were read to the ship's company when the ship commissioned and once a fortnight, usually after divine service. To ensure orders were understood and obeyed instantly, the navy enforced strict discipline. It was accepted as an essential part of a seaman's life. Any misinterpretation of these rules or orders could mean defeat, damage or loss of the ship, and loss of life, injury or illness to the men. Furthermore, the system provided social control and order, moulding a wide range of inexperienced and undisciplined characters in a confined lifestyle where men lived and worked shoulder to shoulder. This code of naval discipline produced a united, ordered and efficient working society that proved its worth in battle.

60. Why were punishments harsh?

Experienced leadership and physical punishment ensured that discipline was maintained. Specific punishments varied according to the offence. They were no more severe at sea than on land. Flogging, where a man could receive from a dozen to five hundred lashes from a cat-of-nine-tails across his bare back, was most common. Officially a captain of a ship could not order a man to receive more than two dozen lashes without authorisation from a higher authority, however, this convention was widely ignored and men could expect three dozen lashes without a court martial. Courts martial were difficult to organise, especially when a ship was operating independently on an isolated patrol. Most ships' captains were fair and practical in the application of discipline, and those who did abuse the system could be dismissed from the service. Execution required the judgement of a court

Cat of nine tails, a boatswain's rattan cane, rope starter & bilboes (leg irons)   Photograph by P Goodwin

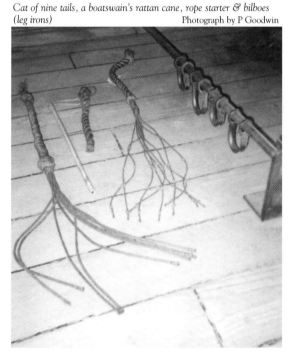

Prison-ship in Portsmouth Harbour with convicts going on board   Illustration by E W Cooke

martial and was reserved for only the most serious offences (desertion, mutiny, murder, 'correspondence with the enemy', cowardice, arson and sodomy). If not hanged, examples were made of serious offenders by having them 'flogged around the fleet', where they would be rowed from ship to ship receiving a number of lashings at each. This could amount to five hundred lashes. Typical flogging offences and severity of punishment were:

Offence	Number of Lashes
Drunkenness	twelve or more if a repeated offence
Theft	thirty-six
Sleeping on duty	six
Disobedience	twenty-four
Filthiness	eighteen
Having wet clothes below decks	twelve

61. What other punishments were there?

For theft, the offender, instead of being flogged, could be forced to 'run the gauntlet'. His shipmates were mustered and formed into two rows ranged around the decks. The offender was then marched between the lines, receiving a severe beating from his shipmates armed with rope ends. For insolence or swearing a man would be gagged with an iron bolt. It was also common for men to be beaten with rattan canes or rope 'starters' by the boatswain's mates or officers if they were considered slow or inefficient in their work. Punishment for boys usually involved caning while tied to a gun, colloquially called 'kissing the gunner's daughter', while unruly midshipmen were either tied in the rigging or sent to the masthead for a long period.

62. What did the crew eat?

Compared to most civilians, seamen in the Royal Navy ate rather well, each man receiving three meals a day. Although the quality of the food varied, especially when ships were at sea for long periods, there was generally plenty of it. On average each seamen received a daily ration containing between three and five thousand calories. This was important, as most work on a man-of-war was labour-intensive. Bread, in the form of ship's biscuit or 'hard tack', had to be softened with water before eating. Fresh vegetables and meat were obtained at every opportunity to supplement the standard victuals. Bad victuals were condemned by a panel of officers, then returned or cast overboard. Daily rations per man:

	Bread lbs	Beer gallons	Beef lbs	Pork lbs	Pease pints	Oatmeal pints	Butter ounces	Cheese ounces
Sunday	1	1		1	fi			
Monday	1	1				1	2	4
Tuesday	1	1	2					
Wednesday	1	1			fi	1	2	4
Thursday	1	1		1	fi			
Friday	1	1			fi	1	2	4
Saturday	1	1	2					
Weekly	7	7	4	2	2	3	6	12
Weekly (metric)	3.2 kg	32 ltr	1.8 kg	.9 kg	1.1 ltr	1.7 ltr	.17 kg	.34 kg

'Launched into eternity'   Illustration by C Field, courtesy of the Royal Marines Museum

Capacity of dry stores carried in Victory:

	tons	tonnes
Salted pork & beef	30	30.60
Pease (peas)	15	15.25
Bread (biscuit) & flour	55	55.86
Butter	2	2.03
Cheese	1	1.02

63. How was food distributed & prepared?

For victualling purposes, the crew was divided into a number of messes, each mess varying between four, six or eight men. One man from each mess was designated cook, responsible for collecting the daily ration of biscuit, meat, peas and vegtables from the ship's steward in the bread room on the orlop deck. The steward, who assisted the purser, carefully measured out each item. The mess cook then returned to his table and prepared the food for

A mess table for eight men set up with square trenchers (wooden plates) & wooden bowls. Ninety tables were needed to feed Victory's crew   Photograph by P Goodwin

Inside the galley pantry   Photograph by P Goodwin

cooking, placed it into a string bag marked with the mess number and took it to the ship's cook in the galley situated on the middle gun deck. Other dry foodstuffs, such as butter and cheese, were retained by the cook to issue to his mess. All the ship's company's food was cooked together on a large fire-hearth called a 'Brodie stove'. Once cooked, each mess cook collected this food in a wooden 'hook pot' and took it back to his mess where the food was shared out. Each mess member took his turn as cook.

64. What was a Brodie Stove?

The type of stove fitted on the ship was invented and patented by a Scotsman, Alexander Brodie, in 1781. Various iron and brick stoves had been used, but Brodie's design proved more suitable and reliable and had a greater cooking capacity than other stoves. Brodie supplied iron stoves to all naval vessels until his death in 1811.

Galley pantry, iron 'Brodie' stove with hanging stoves & copper distiller   Photograph by P Goodwin

At the fore end were two coppers for boiling food, one of 250 gallons, the other of 150 gallons. At the other end was a grate for grilling. In between were two ovens in which eighty pounds of bread could be baked. It had seven external 'hanging stoves' for cooking separate meals for the admiral and officers. There was also a distiller which converted sea water into a small quantity of fresh water. Another unique feature was that spits were automatically rotated by a chain, gear wheel and shaft, operated the smoke-jack. Spare plates and bolts were carried on board for repairs. The stove was generally fuelled with coal, but as only fifty tons were carried on board, this was supplemented with wood collected on shore at every opportunity.

65. Where was livestock kept?

To supplement meat supplies a considerable amount of livestock was embarked when a ship first sailed from port. This included oxen, sheep, pigs, goats and poultry. It was not uncommon for a ship to sail with twelve head of cattle or thirty head of sheep. Although some animals may have been kept in the manger on the lower gun deck, most were corralled in temporary pens situated on the upper gun deck. Poultry (chickens, geese and ducks) were generally kept in coops placed on the forecastle, quarter deck, or in the ships boats. The ship's carpenter, Mr Bunce, recorded that ninety feet of timber was used to make a sheep pen when *Victory* prepared to sail from Portsmouth for Trafalgar. Later, he records that eight empty chicken coops were thrown overboard when *Victory* cleared for action before the battle of Trafalgar.

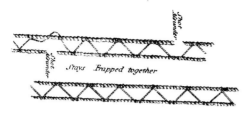

Stays lapped together

66. What did the crew drink?

The main beverages were water, beer, rum and wine. Brandy, Madeira and port were carried for officers, usually at their own expense. The ship could carry up to 300 tons (304.8 tonnes) of water. This equates to 675,000 gallons (3,037,500 litres). Water was kept in large casks called leaguers stored in the lower level of the hold. Unfortunately water did not keep well at sea, becoming fœtid and unfit to drink after a month or so, therefore fresh water was embarked at every opportunity. This was done by carrying empty casks in boats for refilling ashore. The most common drink was beer, each man receiving one gallon (4.5 litres) per day. The maximum capacity of beer carried was fifty tons (50.8 tonnes). The alternative ration to beer was either two pints (1.12 litres) of wine or a half pint (0.28 litres) of rum or brandy. At breakfast the seamen and marines often received a non-alcoholic beverage called 'scotch coffee'. This comprised charred ship's biscuit, crushed and boiled with water and sweetened with a little sugar.

Galley skylight & chicken coops, upper gun deck   Photograph by P Goodwin

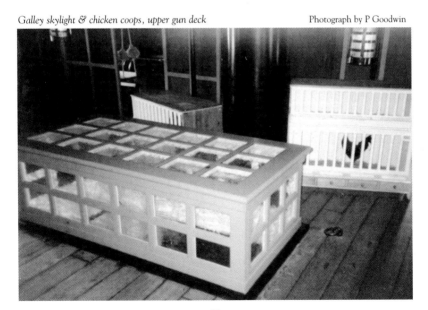

67. What was grog?

Originally a half pint (0.28 litres) of neat rum was issued as an alternative to beer in ships serving in the West Indies. It was falsely believed that rum prevented scurvy. Obviously, this amount of neat rum was very strong and resulted in drunkenness on board ships. Disturbed by the escalating problem, Admiral Vernon, commander-in-chief in the West Indies, decided the rum issue should be diluted. On 21 August 1740 he issued an order that the daily ration of rum would be diluted with one quart (1.14 litres) of water and that it was '...to be mixed in a scuttle butt kept for that purpose, and to be done upon the deck, and in the presence of the Lieutenant of the Watch, who is to take particular care to see the men are not defrauded in having their full allowance of rum, and when so mixed it is to be served to them in two servings in the day, the one between the hours 10 and 12 in the morning, and the other between 4 and 6 in the afternoon.' Vernon's order gradually became general throughout the fleet. The word 'grog' came from the foul-weather or 'grogram' coat that Vernon often wore. He was affectionately nicknamed 'Old Grogram'.

68. What was scurvy?

Scurvy was primarily caused by a deficiency of vitamin C in an unbalanced diet containing too much salted meat, cheese and biscuit, together with a lack of fresh vegetables. It first caused general weakness, stiffness in the joints and skin disorders. When more severe, it resulted in loss of teeth and hair, total weakness and the inability to move, after which victims deterio-

Sick berth & cots at the fore end of upper gun deck viewed from aft   Photograph by P Goodwin

Dispensary & surgeon's table in sick berth, fore end of upper gun deck
By kind permission of the Commanding Officer HMS *Victory*

rated rapidly and died. Towards the end of the eighteenth century shipboard diet was improved by more fresh vegetables and fruit and a daily issue of lemon or lime juice. While credit for these preventive methods has been given to prominent doctors James Lind, Sir Gilbert Blane and Thomas Trotter, effective control of scurvy had been well known since the sixteenth century voyages of John Hawkins and were later adopted by James Cook and Willam Bligh, commander of *Bounty*. Scurvy was not limited to seamen. It was quite common to find the disease in new recruits or pressed men entering the navy, suggesting that the diet on land, especially during the winter, was on occasion equally deficient.

69. Where were sick or injured men cared for?

A specially designated sick berth was fitted on the starboard side of the upper gun deck underneath the forecastle. This area, consisting of a ward and dispensary, was divided by canvas and wooden screens. Here men suffering from disease or injury could be isolated from the cramped confines of the lower deck, and more importantly, from the rest of the crew, to prevent contagion. For practical reasons there were many advantages for placing the sick berth up on this deck. These were fresh air, nearby toilet facilities, warmth and a ready supply of hot water from the galley. Until about 1800, although separated, the sick had been confined on the lower gun deck with the rest of the crew, where sickness could spread quickly.

Midshipmen's mess in the after cockpit of the orlop prepared for battle as a casualty station

Photograph by P Goodwin

70. Where were the wounded treated during battle?

When *Victory* went into battle, the entire sick berth fitted under the fore-castle was dismantled and removed, to permit guns in that area to operate. To treat the wounded, the surgeon set up a temporary hospital in the after cockpit on the orlop deck. This location was also near the main dispensary. Here, in relative safety below the gun decks and gunfire, the wounded were brought and laid on canvas spread out on the deck to await the surgeon. Contrary to popular belief, the deck of the orlop was not painted red to hide the blood. Operations were carried out in the 'action emergency operating theatre' set up on the midshipmen's mess tables and sea chests. Because this area was cramped and dimly lit, treatment under these conditions was crude. Using little or no anaesthetic, the surgeon and his mates carried out amputations and removed splinters and musket shot. After amputation, the stumps of limbs were sealed with spirits of turpentine. Warmed tar was used as a last resort. Surgeons had to be very efficient. In battle conditions, they could amputate a limb in one and a half minutes, but anaesthetic and after-care were non-existent. Sadly, many men died from shock, loss of blood or awaiting surgery.

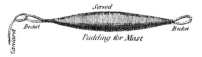

71. What uniforms were worn in the Royal Navy in 1805?

An official full dress and undress uniform for the officers and midshipmen had existed since 1747, albeit with modifications, especially in the 1790s. No official uniform for the 'lower deck' was introduced until 1857, but seamen's clothing was standardised by 1805. This was mainly for practical reasons of living and working at sea. Trousers had wide legs which enabled them to be rolled up easily when scrubbing decks, while jackets were tight-fitting and short-waisted, without tails, which would have encumbered men when aloft in the rigging. Most seamen's clothing was obtained from slops.

72. What were slops?

Slops was the collective name given to clothing provided for seamen by the purser who kept official accounts of clothing issued, the costs of which were deducted from each seaman's pay. Slops were held in a special clothing store situated next to the purser's cabin on the orlop deck. The clothing issued was chosen for its practicality at sea. In general seamen wore the following:

Trousers - white or blue jean or duck, occasionally knee length breeches
Shirts - linen or jersey, red or blue chequered pattern or plain white
Shoes - usually black with silver buckles
Sea boots - if worn, knee length leather
Stockings - wool or silk
Headwear - sennet (straw) or felt hat, Dutch cap with flaps for foul weather
Long apron - protective garment of felt or leather
Belt - leather with sheath for a knife
Neckerchief - black silk
Short jacket - usually blue with brass buttons
Waistcoat - red, yellow or striped kersey
Foul weather coat - rug or frieze

Fore end of the middle gun deck showing one gun lashed for sea & another hoisted to effect repairs to the carriage   Photograph by P Goodwin

Allocation of manpower at quarters

Lower gun deck: thirty 32 pounders

2nd lieutenant	1
6th lieutenant	1
Midshipmen	4
Mates	2
Quarter gunners	4
Gun captains - one per two guns	15
Gun crew - fourteen per two guns[23]	195
Total	222

Middle gun deck: twenty-eight 24 pounders

3rd lieutenant	1
7th lieutenant	1
Midshipmen	4
Mates	1
Quarter gunners	4
Gun captains - one per two guns	14
Gun crew - eleven per two guns	154
Total	179

Upper gun deck: thirty 12 pounders

4th lieutenant	1
8th lieutenant	1
Midshipmen	4
Mates	1
Quarter gunners	4
Gun captains - one per two guns	15
Gun crew - nine per two guns	135
Total	161

Quarter Deck: twelve 12 pounders

Captain	1
Master	1
1st lieutenant	1
Midshipmen	4
Aides de camp & clerks	3
Quartermaster	1
Quartermaster's mates	5
Gun captains - one per two guns	6
Gun crew - nine per two guns	54
Total	76

Forecastle: two 12 pounder guns &
two 68 pounder carronades

9th lieutenant	1
Boatswain	1
Midshipmen	2
Mates	1
Gun captain - one per two 12 pdr guns	1
Gun crew - nine per two 12 pdr guns	9
Gun captain - one per two carronades	1
Gun crew - eight per two carronades	8
Total	24

Poop deck:

5th lieutenant	1
Captain of marines	1
1st lieutenant of marines	1
2nd lieutenant of marines	1
3rd lieutenant of marines	1
Sergeant of marines	1
Marines	8
Total[24]	14

For signals on quarter deck & poop deck:

Midshipmen	3
Clerks	3
Mates	1
Seamen	6
Total	13

Aloft:

Captain of the fore top	1
Fore top men	2
Captain of the main top	1
Main top men	2
Mizzen top men	2
Boatswain's mates & seamen for rigging	14
Total	22

Magazines & handling powder:

Grand magazine:	gunner	1
	gunner's mates	4
	cooper	1
Lightrooms:	master-at-arms	1
	cook & supply	2
Fore hanging magazine:	yeoman	1
	landsmen	2
After hanging magazine:	yeoman	1
	landsmen	2
Fore hatchway:	landsmen & boys	17
Main hatchway:	landsmen & boys	23
After hatchway:	landsmen & boys	26
	Total	81

Orlop: cockpit, well, wings & storerooms:

Surgeon	1
Assistant surgeon	1
Surgeons assistants & loblolly boys	5
Purser	1
Chaplin	1
Carpenter's & Boatswain's storerooms	2
Gunner's & Purser's storerooms	2
Well & wings: carpenter	1
Carpenter's mates & crew	14
Total	28
Grand Total	820

Data compiled by P Goodwin

Millennium Lights: the new illuminations around HMS Victory are switched on for the first time
Chrysalis Picture Library

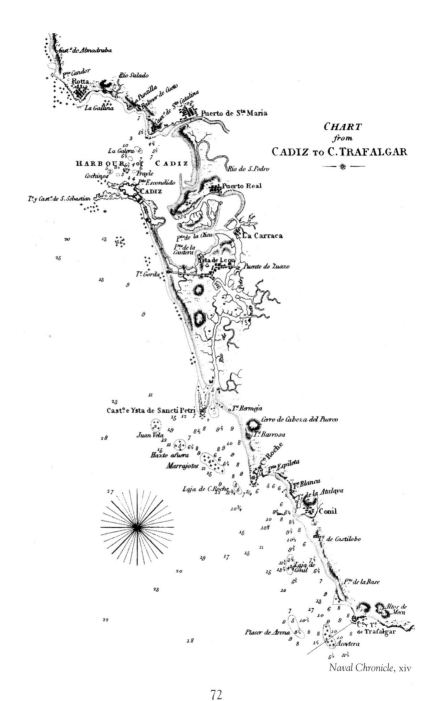

CHART
from
CADIZ TO C. TRAFALGAR

Cast.º de Almadraba

Pta Candor

Rotta

Rio Salado

La Gallina

Peñilla

Polmer de Cueto

Torre de Sta Catalina

Puerto de Sta Maria

Rio de S.Pedro

La Galera

HARBOUR OF CADIZ

Cochinos

Frayle

Pta Escondido

CADIZ

Pta de la Chica

La Carraca

Puerto Real

Tr y Castº de S. Sebastian

Pta de la Cantera

Ysta de Leon

Puente de Xuaxo

Tr Gorda

Castº e Ysta de Sancti Petri

Tr Bermeja

Cerro de Cabeza del Puerco

Juan Vela

Tr Barrosa

Baxte afuera

Roche

Pta Espideta

Marrajotes

Laja de C.Roche

Tr Blanca

Tr de la Atalaya

Conil

Tr de Castilobo

Laja de Conil

Pta de la Base

Altos de Meca

C. Tr de Trafalgar

Placer de Arena

Acevtera

The battle of Trafalgar at about 3.30 pm, Royal Sovereign in centre & Victory on right

Courtesy of the Royal Marines Museum

Nelson, Trafalgar & Victory

73. Where is Trafalgar?

Cape Trafalgar, with its treacherous shoals, lies about 27 miles (34.5 km) SSE of the seaport of Cadiz situated on the south western seaboard of Spain and 40 miles (64.4 km) west of Gibraltar. Trafalgar originates from the Arabic 'Taraf al Agar'.

74. Who commanded the British fleet at Trafalgar?

The overall commander was Vice-Admiral Lord Nelson, KB. His flagship was HMS *Victory*, a first rate ship of the line of 100 guns (actual armament was 104 guns). Her captain was Thomas Masterman Hardy.

75. When & where was Nelson born?

Horatio Nelson was born on Friday 29 September 1758 at Burnham Thorpe, Norfolk. He was the sixth of eleven children born to the Reverend Edmund Nelson and his wife Catherine. Nelson was christened on 9 October 1758 at All Saints Church in Burnham Thorpe where his father was Rector.

Lord Cuthbert Collingwood

76. Who was second in command of the British fleet?

Nelson's second-in-command was Vice-Admiral Cuthbert Collingwood, a Northumbrian, who carried his flag on the 100 gun *Royal Sovereign*. His captain was Edward Rotherham. On Nelson's death Collingwood assumed command of the fleet but, due to damage to *Royal Sovereign* he transferred his flag to the frigate *Euryalus*.

77. Who was supreme commander of the Franco-Spanish fleet?

Overall commander was Vice-Admiral Pierre Villeneuve. His flagship was the 80 gun *Bucentaure*, commanded by Captain Jean-Jacques Magendie. Villeneuve commanded one of the few ships, *Le Guillaume Tell*, to have escaped Nelson's great victory at the battle of the Nile, 1 August 1798.

'Dismasted, but not defeated': the 74 gun Belleisle, commanded by Captain William Hargood, at Trafalgar 21 October 1805   Illustration by C Field courtesy of the Royal Marines Museum

After the battle Belleisle was taken in tow by Naiad frigate, 39 guns, commanded by Captain Thomas Dundas   Illustration by C Field, courtesy of the Royal Marines Museum

78. Who was senior Spanish admiral at Trafalgar?

Second-in-command of the combined Franco-Spanish fleet was Admiral Fredrico Carlos Gravina. His flagship was the 112 gun *Principe de Asturias*.

79. What was the overall strength of opposing fleets at Trafalgar?

Fleet	Ships	Guns	Men
British	27	2,148	17,000
Franco- Spanish	33	2,632	30,000
Difference	6	484	13,000

The above figures exclude smaller ships not fully engaged in the battle:

Fleet	Frigates	Brigs	Schooners	Armed Cutters
British	4	0	1	1
Franco-Spanish	7	3	0	0

80. Who shot Nelson?

Lord Nelson was shot by a French sharpshooter stationed in the mizzen mast of the 74 gun *Rédoutable* commanded by the very able Captain Jean-Jacques Lucas. This French ship was at the time heavily engaged fighting alongside the starboard side of *Victory*. According to *Victory's* logbook, the fatal shot was fired at 1.15 pm. Nelson was carried below from the quarter deck to the cockpit on the orlop where he died of his wounds at about 4.30 pm after receiving the news that he had gained a great victory. His age at the time of death was forty-seven years, three weeks and one day.

81. What were Nelson's last words?

His last words are a subject of considerable controversy. Upon receiving his wound, Lord Nelson was heard to say: 'They have done for me at last, Hardy. My backbone is shot through.' As he lay dying in the orlop, he said 'Oh Victory! Victory! how you distract my poor brain.' According to several witnesses, his final order was: 'Anchor, Hardy, anchor.' Although he did say 'Kiss me, Hardy', they could not have been his last words as the captain was on deck when the admiral died. Dr Beatty insisted that before the 'matchless hero' slipped into delirium, he declared: 'I have done my duty. I praise God for it'.[25]

82. How many casualties were suffered?

Among British ships, Victory sustained the highest casualties. Including Nelson, 57 were killed and 102 were wounded. This equates to 6.9 per cent and 12.42 per cent of her complement respectively:

Fleet	Total men	Dead	%	Wounded	%	Total	%
British	17,000	449	2.64	1,214	7.14	1,663	9.78
Combined Fleet[26]	30,000	4,408	14.69	2,545	8.48	6,953	23.18
Total	47,000	4,857	10.33	3,759	7.99	8,616	18.33

83. Which ships were captured or destroyed?

No British ships were captured or destroyed. Opposition losses were:

Fleet	Total Ships	Captured	%	Blown up	%	Total	%
French	18	8	44.4	1	5.5	9	50
Spanish	15	9	60.0	0	0	9	60
Total	33	17	51.5	1	3.0	18	

Of the remaining French ships, four vessels, Formidable, Duguay-Trouin, Mont-Blanc and Scipion under Admiral Dumanoir escaped. All were captured two weeks later off Cape Viñano by a British squadron commanded by Admiral Richard Strachan. Five ships, Pluton, Héros, Neptune, Argonaute and Indomitable, sailed back to Cadiz. These were later joined by Algéciras, which was recaptured from the British.

Of the remaining Spanish ships, five vessels, San Francisco de Asís, Montañés, Rayo, San Leandre and San Justo, led by Admiral Gravina in the Príncipe de Asturias sailed for Cadiz. These were later joined by Santa Ana which was recaptured from the British. Of the thirteen ships that sailed from Cadiz, only ten arrived. The other three, San Francisco de Asís, Montañés and Rayo, were lost in the gale that followed the battle.

Only four of the seventeen British prizes actually reached Gibraltar. Two were recaptured (Algéciras and Santa Ana), the others sank, ran ashore on the rocky coastline, or were scuttled (sunk) en route, due to their battle-damaged condition. Obviously these losses greatly reduced the expected amount of prize money due to those who fought at Trafalgar.

84. What happened to Victory after the battle?

Victory was heavily damaged. She lost most of her masts, rigging and a considerable proportion of her upperworks. There were fires on the forecastle, skid beams and orlop deck in the after cockpit, near the after hanging magazine. On 24 October she was taken under tow by Polyphemus (64) but soon parted company and was left to weather the storm on her own. After the gales subsided she was finally taken in tow by Neptune (98) and arrived at Gibraltar on 28 October. After temporary repairs she sailed for England, arriving at Portsmouth on 4 December. The ship then proceeded to Chatham where she went into dock on 6 January 1806 for a major refit.

85. What happened to Nelson's body?

The day after the battle his body was, with the exception of his shirt, stripped of all clothing and examined by Victory's surgeon, William Beatty. Preserving the corpse for the journey home presented a problem. However Dr Beatty devised a clever plan. Nelson's body was placed into a large water cask, called a leaguer. It was then filled with brandy - a spirit known for its preservation qualities. Apertures were made at the top and bottom of the cask to permit removal and replenishment of fluid. The leaguer was placed upright on the middle deck under the charge of a marine sentinel where it remained until the ship reached Gibraltar. There it was found that the body had absorbed a quantity of the brandy. This was replaced with spirits of wine, the best fluid available for preservation. On 3 November Victory sailed for England. Due to adverse weather, the passage took four and a half weeks, and the cask was refilled twice with two parts brandy to one part spirits of wine. On 4 December the ship anchored at St Helens near Portsmouth. On 11 December Victory sailed to Chatham for repairs and Nelson's body was removed from the leaguer and examined for decay by Beatty. During the examination Beatty removed the fatal musket ball, complete with part of Nelson's epaulette. The body was then wrapped in a cotton vestment and bandages and placed into a lead coffin filled with brandy and a solution of camphor and myrrh. This lead coffin was put inside a wooden casket and placed in Nelson's day cabin. On the 21 December the Admiralty ordered the removal of Nelson's corpse to Greenwich. The body was removed from the lead coffin and placed in a wooden casket made from the mainmast of the French ship l'Orient which had blown up during Nelson's great victory at the Nile. This casket was a gift to Nelson from Captain Benjamin Hallowell. It was placed inside another lead coffin, which was soldered up and placed inside a wooden shell. On 22 December, off Sheerness, the entire casket was transferred to Chatham yacht (belonging to Commissioner Grey, senior dockyard official at Chatham), for transportation up river to Greenwich. Here Beatty carried out a full autopsy.

86. When was Nelson's funeral & where was he buried?

Nelson's body laid in state within the Painted Hall at Greenwich Hospital between 5 and 7 January 1806. On the 8th the coffin was transferred to Charles II's state barge and taken upstream to Whitehall, accompanied by a cavalcade of river craft. On arrival at Whitehall, the body was taken to Admiralty Buildings and placed in a small room overnight. The state funeral took place the next day, with thousands of people lining the streets along the procession route between Whitehall and St Paul's Cathedral. At noon the grand procession left the Admiralty. Nelson's body was carried on an open hearse decked out to resemble his flagship *Victory* and drawn by six horses. The funeral car was followed by the chief mourners and sixty seamen and marines from *Victory*. Attending the procession was Admiral Villeneuve who had been granted parole for this occasion. (He died under mysterious circumstances when he returned to France). Finally the cortège reached St Paul's, where a grand service was attended by royalty, state officials, a host of admirals, captains and Nelson's estranged wife Fanny. At about 5.30 pm the ceremony drew to a close and Nelson's body was lowered into the crypt. Both original coffins were now encased in a stone sarcophagus once intended for Henry VIII's chancellor, Cardinal Wolsey, over which was draped the union flag. As the sarcophagus was being lowered into the crypt, *Victory's* seamen, forgetting the gravity of the occasion, rushed forward and tore pieces from the ensign and stuffed them into their pockets. This was an emotional, yet understandable gesture by the men who knew and loved their hero best.

Nelson's funeral car bedecked to represent the Victory   *Naval Chronicle, xv*

Victory in Portsmouth harbour circa 1886, viewed from Gosport

Victory flying the court-martial jack during the Cobra court-martial[27]

Illustration by C Field, courtesy of the Royal Marines Museum

Victory after Trafalgar

87. What rôle did Victory serve after Trafalgar?

Arriving at Chatham Dockyard on 16 January 1806, Victory was paid off (de-commissioned). Most of her crew was transferred into Ocean. After rigging, stores and guns had been removed Victory was taken into dock on 6 March for extensive repairs. When re-commissioned in March 1808 her armament was reduced to ninety-eight guns and she was reclassified as a second rate ship. For the next four years her rôle varied, serving in the Baltic under Admiral James Saumarez and supporting the Peninsular Wars. In 1808, Victory sailed for the Baltic to assist Sweden. In the winter of the same year she was sent as a troop ship to La Coruña, to embark the remaining forces of Sir John Moore's defeated army, arriving home on 23 January 1809. Returning to the Baltic, she took part in the blockade of the Russian fleet at Kronstadt, then she underwent some minor repairs at Portsmouth in 1810. Temporarily fitted out as a troop ship in 1811, she was sent to Lisbon, trans-porting the first battalion of the 36th Regiment of Foot to support Sir Arthur Wellesley (later the Duke of Wellington) in his Peninsular campaign to drive the French out of Spain. Again, under the flag of Saumarez, the ship was sent to the Baltic and remained on station off Wingo Sound until her final return home in December 1812.

88. When did her career as a fighting ship end?

Her last voyage brought her back into Portsmouth on 4 December 1812, where she was finally paid off from active service. Now forty-seven years old (coincidentally, the same age as Nelson at his death), the ship was in need of considerable repair work. Surveyed at Portsmouth dockyard in 1813, Victory was 'taken in hand' and put into dock where she underwent a 'great repair' between the years 1814 and 1816. During this period her stern and bow were modified, her ornamentation reduced and many of her knees were replaced with wooden chocks and iron plate knees. Her upperworks were also altered. With the final defeat of Napoleon at Waterloo on 18 June 1815, any hopes of Victory continuing her service as a fighting ship were finished. From 1816 until 1824 she was laid up in ordinary (reserve). After this date she became the flagship to the Port Admiral. In 1869 she became the ten-der to another ship, Duke of Wellington. In 1889 she became the flagship of the Commander-in-Chief, Naval Home Command. Her position remains unaltered today except that now she acts as flagship to the Second Sea Lord/Commander-in-Chief, Naval Home Command, thus making her the oldest commissioned warship in the world.

Fishermens Bend

'Victory's narrow escape'　　　　　　Illustration by C Field, courtesy of the Royal Marines Museum

89. What happened to Victory in 1903?

Victory was accidentally rammed by the iron battleship *Neptune*, which was being towed to a breaker's yard in Germany. The incident occurred when the tow line parted, with the result that *Neptune's* bow smashed into the port side of *Victory* at the spot where Nelson was assumed to have died. The hole made in the side of the ship at the waterline was three by seven feet (one by

Damage caused by Neptune in 1903　　　By kind permission of the Commanding Officer HMS *Victory*

82

Victory being towed from her mooring to No 1 Basin - January 1922   Courtesy of Mr S Humphreys

two metres). Leaking badly, *Victory* was immediately docked for repairs. Ironically, the ship causing the accident bore the same name as the ship that had saved and towed *Victory* to Gibraltar after the battle of Trafalgar. *Victory* was also damaged by a 250 pound bomb during a heavy bombing raid in World War Two.

The 'eyes of the fleet', a frigate under full sail   E W Cooke, 1828

Victory in No 1 Basin waiting to go into No 2 Dock for restoration, January 1922
By kind permission of the Commanding Officer HMS *Victory*

The divers who raised Victory when George V indicated she was too low in Number 2 Dock
By kind permission of the Commanding Officer HMS Victory

'Save the Victory' campaign & restoration

90. When was Victory placed in her present dock?

The ship was brought into No 2 dock on 12 January 1922. Shortly afterwards, King George V visited and gestured that she should be higher. The task involved building a concrete base underwater to raise the ship so that her natural waterline was level with the dockside. Work then commenced to restore the ship to her 1805 Trafalgar configuration. This involved reconstructing her bow and stern and making several internal alterations. It was also necessary to replace most of her masts and rigging and re-arm the ship with replica guns, as most had been removed many years before.

91. Who has been responsible for her restoration?

In 1910 the Society for Nautical Research (SNR) was formed to encourage research into seafaring and shipbuilding of all nations. The SNR also addressed concerns regarding *Victory's* survival. She was now very old and her hull was in a bad condition, but no action was taken until after World War I. After the war, the ship was moved into her present dock to be restored to her Trafalgar appearance. Supported by the Royal Navy, Portsmouth Dockyard workers and facilities, the work was completed in five years and *Victory* was opened to the public in 1928.

Victory celebrating the centenary of the battle of Trafalgar, 21 October 1905. Alongside is B1, one of the Royal Navy's earliest submarines   By kind permission of the Commanding Officer HMS *Victory*

92. How much did the initial restoration cost?

On Trafalgar Day 1922 the Society for Nautical Research campaigned to raise funds for the ship's restoration, introducing the 'Save the Victory Fund'. In 1923, public donations were boosted with a gift of £50,000 from Sir James Caird and by 1931 a total of £105,000 had been received.

93. How is the work managed?

The overall restoration is controlled by the Victory Advisory Technical Committee which instructs skilled shipwrights in repairing the hull. Twenty shipwrights, riggers and painters form an in-house workforce for the naval base. All internal restoration, visual interpretation, rigging and historical research is undertaken or overseen by Victory's curator.

94. What types of timber are used in restoration?

While the ship was originally constructed from oak, suitable sizes of this timber are now scarce and expensive. Teak and iroko are used as alternatives. Internal and minor works are generally made from pine.

Quarter deck, starboard battery of short 12 pounder guns   Photograph by P Goodwin

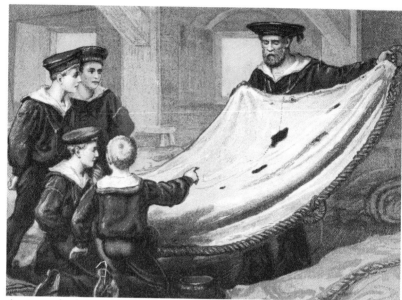

A veteran sailor shows young boys Victory's battle-torn fore topsail in Chatham sail loft circa 1880
Author's collection

95. Where is cordage for rigging obtained?

All cordage for rigging and other requirements throughout the ship is man-ufactured at the ropewalk in Chatham Historic Dockyard. This ropery, run as a private business, uses all the original equipment that has been opera-tional for at least 230 years. Operating as a working museum, the Ropery at Chatham is open to the public today. Similarly, flags used for the signals are produced in a flag loft at Chatham Dockyard.

96. What related conservation projects are being undertaken?

Besides the ship, the biggest conservation project currently undertaken relates to the original fore topsail used on *Victory* at the battle of Trafalgar. Measuring 54 feet (16.45 m) across its head, 54 feet (16.45 m) deep and 70 feet (21.33 m) across its foot, the sail has an area of about 320 square yards (268 sq m). This fore topsail is riddled with some ninety shot holes and rents caused by enemy gunfire at the battle. It is hoped to exhibit the sail perma-nently within the next few years. Due to the condition of the sail, the ship's curator and textile conservator, Sharon Manitta, must carry out careful research to develop the display of this historic textile. The flax canvas for this sail was woven in Dundee, Scotland.

Clue of a Sail

The recovery of *Victory*'s fore topsail was revealed in the *Chatham News* on 13 May 1893. Their reporter, John Thompson, a former shipwright at Chatham Dockyard, was told that if he visited the sail loft stores, he would 'find an interesting relic unknown to the present authorities, or to the public'. This relic proved to be *Victory*'s fore and main topsails, deposited since the 'memorable battle' of Trafalgar. The sails were stretched out on drying posts, where the main topsail was found to be 'riddled with leaden balls of musketry, 315 in number, the fore topsail's bolt rope was also completely shattered by a great number of shot holes', while 'streaks and spots of human blood could be plainly seen in the centre of the sail.' The Royal Engineers photographed the sails and the Port Admiral at Portsmouth requested 'that these relics be sent there, so as to be exhibited on board that noble ship the *Victory*'. While the fore topsail is currently undergoing restoration, sadly the main topsail disappeared during World War II.[28]

Temporary exhibition of Victory's battle-torn fore topsail with ninety shot holes, International Festival of the Sea, Portsmouth 1998　　　　　　　　　　Photograph by P Goodwin

Trundlehead of the main capstan with messenger cable turned around the whelps
By kind permission of the Commanding Officer HMS *Victory*

Drumhead of the jeer capstan used to bring on stores, boats, guns & raise masts and lower yards on their jeer tackle
By kind permission of the Commanding Officer HMS *Victory*

Victory today: flagship & public attraction

97. Victory is still in commission. What does this mean?

A commissioned ship is a vessel listed as an operational warship by the national navy of the country concerned. In the case of *Victory*, the Royal Navy still flies its white ensign at her stern. *Victory* serves as the flagship of the Second Sea Lord/Commander-in-Chief Naval Home Command and wears the Admiral's flag at the masthead. Although not a fighting ship, the ship's daily running is governed by a lieutenant commander. His staff includes a first lieutenant, chief petty officers and seamen ratings. To fulfil her rôle as a museum, *Victory* is also staffed with civilian personnel: a curator, a visitor services manager, a corps of guides and an industrial support team. Because *Victory* has been in commission since 1778 she is the oldest commissioned warship in the world. Second to this is the 44-gun American frigate USS *Constitution*, 'Old Ironsides', commissioned in 1797.

'An olive branch.' HMS Implacable (formerly Duguay Trouin - named after a St Malo corsair)
Illustration by C Field, courtesy of the Royal Marines Museum

98. Did any other Trafalgar ships survive into the twentieth century?

Yes, the French 74 gun ship *Duguay Trouin*, launched at Rochefort in 1800. Although this ship escaped at the battle of Trafalgar, she was later captured off Cape Viñano on 3 November 1805 by Admiral Sir Richard Strachan. Refitted, the ship was renamed *Implacable* and entered the Royal Navy. After fifty years of sea service, she was hulked as a training ship at Plymouth. As part of the 1905 centenary celebrations, an offer was made to return this Trafalgar veteran to France, but it was declined. In 1911 *Implacable* was given to Wheatley Cobb as a training ship for sea scouts based at Falmouth. She was later moved to Portsmouth along with the training ship *Foudroyant* (ex-44 gun frigate *Trincomalee*, built in Bombay 1817, but now restored and open to the public at Hartlepool). No longer used for training, *Implacable* was brought into Portsmouth Dockyard in the late 1930s and used as a store-ship. A plan to restore the ship and put her into a dry dock at Greenwich (now occupied by the tea clipper *Cutty Sark*) failed. Wrongly considered beyond restoration, the ship was condemned and scuttled in the Channel off the Owers on 2 December 1949. She sank wearing both the British naval white ensign and tricolour of France. Besides various artefacts, some bulk-head panelling from *Implacable* is held on board the preserved 44 gun frigate *Unicorn* (1824) at Dundee. The entire stern section, complete with its ornate carvings, can now be seen at the National Maritime Museum, Greenwich.

99. How many people visit Victory each year?

Victory is open to the public all year except Christmas Day. On average the ship receives 360,000 visitors annually, with figures rising to 2,500 a day in the summer. Besides Europeans, visitors come from Japan, Australia and the United States. Ironically, some 20,000 French and Spanish tourists visit each year. In addition, the Royal Navy invites many guests, including heads of state, royalty and foreign diplomats. Often they are entertained in the unique surroundings of Nelson's great cabin. Tours are conducted by the corps of Victory guides. To assist foreign visitors, they provide guided scripts in twenty-one languages.

100. Who are the Victory guides?

The majority of the people forming the corps of Victory guides are retired naval and royal marine personnel who conduct public tours around the ship. Officially established on 1 October 1990, this corps of civil servants replaced the naval ratings previously used. The objective of this change was to create a professional group of museum-grade guides to provide better and consistent expertise to meet the requirements of today's paying public. The first female guide started in April 2000.

101. Where is the Victory Gallery?

The Victory Gallery in the nearby Royal Naval Museum provides, through artefacts, paintings and displays, the story of Victory and the battle of Trafalgar. It also describes and illustrates the construction and restoration history of the ship. It features the spectacular battle of Trafalgar diorama by W L Wyllie, RA, and a multi-media recreation of the battle itself. The gallery also displays Charles II's state barge used for Nelson's funeral.

Through exhibits, models, paintings and artefacts, this museum also tells the story of the Royal Navy from its beginning to the present day. There are two new galleries, one dedicated to Nelson, HMS Victory & the Battle of Trafalgar and one tracing the history of the Sailing Navy. The museum also holds a unique collection of photographs and documents related to the Royal Navy with the recent addition of the Admiralty Library. Research facilities are available to the public during normal weekday opening hours.

Bale Slings

Can Hook Slings

Hook   Hook

Hitcher   Thimble

Hogs or Butt Slings

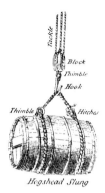

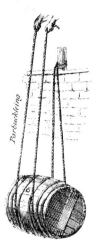

Hogshead Slung

Cask Slung

Endnotes

[1] Literally, 'marvellous year'.

[2] Dockyard reserve, paid from 'ordinary' rather than 'extraordinary' estimate of the navy.

[3] Rosin is a lacquer obtained after distilling the oil from crude turpentine.

[4] Hume & Smollett, *History of England* (London: 1860), iii.

[5] *Ibid.*

[6] This internal measurement is taken from the underside of the lower gun deck planking to the inner planking near the centre of the hold thereby excluding the orlop deck, the orlop not being classified as a proper deck in the true sense.

[7] Rough rule of thumb for building men-of-war: one acre per gun.

[8] All the portraits on these two pages are from the *Naval Chronicle* - Keppel (vii, 277), Parker (xx, 337), Kempenfelt (vii, 365), Howe (ix, 396), Hood (xi, 400), Jervis (iv, 1), Nelson (iii, 167), Saumarez (vi, 85), courtesy of the Royal Marines Museum.

[9] PRO ADM 95/39, Observations of the Quality of His Majesty's Ship *Victory*, 1797.

[10] The bronze 42 pounders were removed by Keppel in 1778 and replaced with 32 pounders. Keppel disliked the 42 pounder due to their weight, slowness to fire and the need for a large gun crew. After he left, the ship's lower deck armament was restored to 42 pounders - only to be replaced with 32 pounders again in 1803.

[11] The term larboard is used in preference to port. The latter was introduced in 1844 to avoid confusion between starboard and larboard when giving orders in heavy weather or noisy conditions. The change was also connected with the introduction of steam navigation.

[12] RNM MSS 1986/573 (11) & MSS 1064/83 (2376).

[13] Ballast, comprising blocks of pig iron and loose shingle, has been omitted from this list as it would often vary in relation to the total provisions carried.

[14] Figures vary according to whether the ship was provisioned for channel or foreign service.

[15] This does not include marines' muskets.

[16] This list has been compiled from the official list of those receiving government grants and prize money. Lord Nelson is not included as he was additional to the ship's complement.

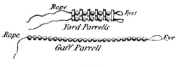

[17] RNM MSS 118, Captain J Sutton's order books, HMS *Egmont* & HMS *Superb*, 1798-1801.

[18] This information is taken from original notes written by William Rivers, gunner in *Victory* at Trafalgar. These documents are now held in the Royal Naval Museum, Portsmouth.

[19] I am indebted to Dr Ann Coats for supplying these comparative statistics.

[20] RNM, MSS 1986/573 (11).

[21] A/size replica of the original figurehead can be seen in the *Victory* Gallery at the Royal Naval Museum.

[22] RNM, MSS 1986/573 (11).

[23] Powder monkeys were not included in gun crews.

[24] The exact number of personnel stationed on the poop deck is unknown. This estimate is based on records indicating that eight marines manning this deck were cut down with a single bar shot.

[25] James, W, *Naval History of Great Britain from the Declaration of War by France in 1793 to the Accession of George IV* (London: 1837), iv, 43, 81-84.

[26] As French and Spanish casualty returns were incomplete, these figures are approximations.

[27] *Cobra* was a new fast destroyer that broke in half during sea trials in 1901. There were questions both about her design and her captain's financial problems at the time of the accident. Singleton, P, 'The loss of HMS *Cobra*', *Naval Historical Research & Collectors Association Review*, Summer 1999, 25-33. Thanks to George Malcolmson for this reference.

[28] The information was kindly supplied by Peter Dawson, editor of *CHIPS*, newsletter of Chatham Dockyard Historical Society.

Russian sailors joining in the centenary celebrations of England's greatest naval triumph, the battle of Trafalgar. Five months earlier, after travelling halfway around the world, their navy suffered its greatest defeat, the battle of Tsushima. By kind permission of the Commanding Officer HMS Victory

Curator confirming the main topgallant truck is 180 feet (54.86 m) above the deck   Photograph by P Goodwin

About the author

Peter Goodwin was born in 1951 in Kensington, but later moved to Tunbridge Wells. Educated at Christchurch School and Sandown Court Secondary Modern School, Peter was both a lifeboy and a sea cadet. Taught to sail by Morin Scott, he developed in a keen interest in ships, began making models and started his first scratch-built 64 gun ship at thirteen. At the same time he had his first taste of sea training in the old frigate *Foudroyant*.

At fifteen Peter joined the Royal Navy at HMS *Ganges* to train as a marine engineering mechanic. For recreation he sailed thirty-two foot cutters. Drafted into the fleet, he served in *Hermes*, *Manxman* and *Droxford*. In 1970 he joined the submarine service, serving in the Polaris nuclear submarine *Resolution*. He began making a museum standard model of a 74 gun ship in 1972. Like *Victory*, it remains a work in progress. In 1976, he undertook a two-year ONC engineering course at HMS *Sultan* to become an engine room artificer, then joining the submarine *Renown*. Rated chief petty officer marine engineering artificer in 1979, he undertook the long nuclear course at HMS *Sultan*, culminating in an HND and Incorporated Engineer qualification. Peter returned to *Renown* for two years. After training with Rolls Royce, he worked as a nuclear standards and quality assurance inspector repairing nuclear systems in submarines at Faslane.

catspaw

On publishing his first book, *The Construction and Fitting of the Sailing Man of War* in 1987, he left the navy to devote more time to research and writing. A second book, *The Anatomy of the 20 Gun Ship Blandford*, followed in 1988 and a third, *The Anatomy of the Bomb Vessel Granado 1742*, in 1989. He was also a senior design engineer at YARD Ltd Engineering Consultants, Glasgow working on the development of nuclear power stations and submarines, and the Faslane shiplift project.

In 1991 Peter published his fourth book, *The Anatomy of the Naval Cutter 1777*, and soon after became the first keeper and curator of HMS *Victory* in 1991. In 1996 he undertook additional duties as secretary of the *Victory* Advisory Technical Committee and began a postgraduate course at the Scottish Institute of Maritime Studies at St Andrew's University, graduating as Master of Philosophy in 1998. His detailed study of *Nelson's Ships* was published in 2002. Besides working as technical and historical adviser on the restoration and interpretation of *Victory*, he has also acted as consultant for HMS *Trincomalee* (formerly *Foudroyant*), the Portuguese *Don Fernando II e Glória*, *Endeavour*, *Grand Turk* and various museum, television and film projects. In his spare time, Peter organises and participates in historical re-enactments and sails in square riggers - including *Royalist*, *Astrid*, *Endeavour* and *Grand Turk*. And, of course, he is hard at work on his next book, *The Ships of Trafalgar*, to be published in 2005.

Quarter deck, short 12 pounder gun & ladder to poop deck   Photograph by P Goodwin

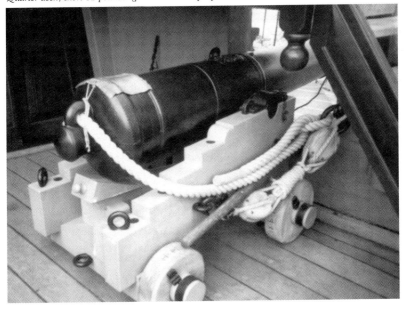

Original grindstone recovered from the wreck of Invincible and mounted in a replica stand Photograph by P Goodwin

Bibliography

Addis C, *The men who fought with Nelson on the Victory at Trafalgar* (Nelson Society: 1988)

Albion, R, *Forests and seapower: the timber problem of the Royal Navy 1652-1862* (Cambridge, MA: 1926)

Beatty, W, *Death of Lord Nelson* (London: 1985)

Beauchant, T, *Naval gunner* (London: 1828)

Boudriot, J, *Seventy-four gun ship* (Rotherfield: 1986)

Brenton, E, *Naval history of Great Britain 1783-1836*, (London: 1837)

Buglar, A, *HMS Victory: building, restoration & repair* (London: 1966)

Callender, G, *The story of HMS Victory* (London: 1914)

Corbett, J, *The campaign of Trafalgar* (London: 1910)

Corbett, J, *Some principles of maritime strategy* (London: 1911)

Desbrière, E, *The naval campaign of 1805* (Paris: 1907), Translated by C Eastwick (Oxford: 1933)

Fenwick, K, *HMS Victory* (London: 1959)

Midshipmans hitch

Fincham, J, *Introductory outline of the practice of shipbuilding* (London: 1821)

Fincham, J, *History of naval architecture* (London: 1851)

Gardiner, R, *The Trafalgar campaign 1803-1805* (London: 1997)

Goodwin, P, *Construction & fitting of the sailing man of war: 1650-1850* (London: 1987)

Goodwin, P, 'The influence of industrial technology & material procurement on the design, construction and development of HMS *Victory* (1765-1830)' (University of St Andrew's : 1998)

Harland, J, *Seamanship in the age of sail* (London: 1984)

Hibbert, C, *Nelson: A personal history* (London: 1994)

Hill, J, *Oxford illustrated history of the Royal Navy* (Oxford: 1995)

Hill, R, *The prizes of war: the naval prize system in the Napoleonic wars 1793-1815* (Portsmouth: 1998)

Howarth, D, *Trafalgar: the Nelson touch* (London: 1969)

Hutchinson, J, *Press gang afloat & ashore* (London: 1913)

James, W, *Naval history of Great Britain from the declaration of war by France in 1793 to the accession of George IV* (London: 1837)

King, D, *Every man will do his duty* (London: 1997)

Cutlass chest, ready for battle   Photograph by P Goodwin

Long 12 pounder, complete with lead gunlock apron & powder horn   Photograph by P Goodwin

Laird Clowes W, *The Royal Navy*, seven volumes (London: 1897)

Lavery, B, *Arming & fitting English ships of war: 1600-1815* (London: 1987)

Lavery, B, *Building the wooden walls* (London: 1989)

Lavery, B, *Nelson's navy: the ships, men & organisation 1793-1815* (London: 1991)

Lavery, B, *Shipboard life & organisation 1731-1815*, vol. 138 (NRS: 1998)

Lees, J, *Masting & rigging of English ships of war: 1625-1860* (London: 1979)

Lever, D, *Young officers' sheet anchor* (London: 1819)

Lloyd, C, *British seaman* (London: 1968)

Longridge, C, *Anatomy of Nelson's ships* (London: 1955)

Lyon, D, *Sea battles in close-up: the age of Nelson* (Shepperton: 1986)

Mahan, *Influence of sea power upon history 1660-1783* (Boston: 1890)

Mathew, D, *British seamen* (London: 1943)

McGowan, A, *HMS Victory: her construction, career & restoration* (London: 1999)

McKay, J, *100 gun ship Victory* (London: 1987)

Morriss, R, *Campaign of Trafalgar* (London: 1997)

Nicolas, N, *The dispatches & letters of Lord Nelson* (London: 1844)

Oman, C, *Nelson* (London: 1947)

Parkinson, C, *Britannia rules* (Stroud: 1994)

Ranft, B McL, *The Vernon papers* (NRS: 1958)

Rodger, N, *Articles of war* (Havant: 1982)

Rodger, N, *Safeguard of the sea* (London: 1997)

Rodger, N, *Wooden world: Anatomy of the Georgian Navy* (London: 1986)

Schom, A, *Trafalgar: countdown to battle 1803-1805* (Oxford: 1990)

Southey, R, *Life of Nelson* (London: 1906)

Steel D, *Elements of mastmaking, sailmaking & rigging* (London: 1794)

Steel D, *Elements & practice of naval architecture* (London: 1804)

Watson, J, *Reign of George III* (Oxford: 1960)

White, C, *The Nelson companion* (Stroud: 1995)

White, C, *1797: Nelson's year of destiny* (Stroud: 1997)

Musket chest, ready for battle, upper gun deck   Photograph by P Goodwin

Outside Clinch

Journals & Periodicals

Carr-Laughton, L, 'HMS Victory', *The Mariner's Mirror*, volume 10, 1924

Feazer, E, 'HMS *Victory*', *The Mariners Mirror*, volume 8, 1922

Jones, A, 'Sir Thomas Slade', *The Mariner's Mirror*, vol 63, 1977

Naval Chronicle, volumes ii, iii, iv, vi, vii, ix, xi, xiv, xv & xx

Nelson Dispatch, Journal of the Nelson Society

Trafalgar Chronicle, Journal of the 1805 Club

Sheepshank

Primary Sources

National Maritime Museum (NMM), *Victory*: Lines as Built, 1759, no 206, box 4, ZAZ.0122

NMM, *Victory*: Profile of the Inboard Works, no 206B, box 4, ZAZ.0122

NMM, *Victory*: Profile of the Inboard Works, VR 179, PS 40/01 Portsmouth Dockyard

Public Record Office (PRO), ADM 180/10, Progress Book (HMS *Victory*)

PRO, ADM 95/39, Observations of the Sailing Qualities of His Majesty's Ship *Victory*, 1797

Royal Naval Museum (RNM), MSS 1998/41, Rivers Papers, Journals of Master Gunner William Rivers in HMS *Victory*, 1793-1811

RNM, MSS 1986/573 (11), Rivers Papers, Journal of Midshipman William Rivers in HMS *Victory*

RNM, MSS 1064/83 2376, Record of Carpenter's and Boatswain's Stores and Expenses for *Victory*, *Britannia*, and *Africa* for the Year 1805, (covers July - December 1805)

RNM, MSS 118, Order book of Captain John Sutton, HMS *Egmont*, 1798-1801 and HMS *Superb*, 1798-1801

Victory Archive, VLDA 2000, Letter and Document Archive, HMS *Victory*

Victory Archive, VPA 2000, Photographic Archive, HMS *Victory*

Jack Knot